GUIDE TO WILD FLOWERS AND TREES

Guide to
WILD FLOWERS
AND TREES

by Peter Hausman

CHICAGO

J. G. FERGUSON AND ASSOCIATES

Preface

In GUIDE TO WILD FLOWERS AND TREES you will find just the information which you need for identifying the many beautiful flowers and trees and other interesting forms of plant life which you come upon in the fields and woods on a short outing near your home or when you are further away on a vacation. The drawings and the articles call to your attention the characteristic and distinctive points about the blossoms or leaves or berries or stems which make recognition easy and certain. In addition, the articles tell you about the habits of the plants, and where you are most likely to find them.

As the title indicates, the book is planned primarily to acquaint the reader with the principal wild flowers and trees. Yet it offers even more, since it includes also the simpler forms of plant life such as mosses and ferns, which you will also want to recognize when you see them on your walks in the woods or fields. By bringing together in one volume all these varied types of plants, the book gives its readers an intimate sense of the close relationship between all forms of plant life.

We take up first the Lowly Plant Life of the Fields and Woods, such as the more common toadstools and mushrooms, and the mosses, lichens, ground pines, and ferns which you are most likely to see. This is followed by Lowly Plant Life of Ponds and Streams.

The next section, Guide to American Wild Flowers, is of course a major division of the book, devoted to the wealth of beauty which the flower world offers us. In order to make it

v

especially easy and convenient to use, we have grouped the wild
flowers according to the kind of location in which they grow.
When you are on an outing, you can therefore turn to the subdivision dealing with the kind of setting in which you happen to
be. The first subdivision is Wild Flowers of Ponds, Marshes, and
Damp Meadows, including such varied favorites as pond lilies,
pickerelweed, arrowheads, skunk cabbage, wild iris, marsh
marigold, cat-tails, spiderwort, meadow rue, fringed gentian, and
many others. Next we take up Wild Flowers of Fields, Pastures,
and Roadsides, where we find clovers, daisies, Queen Anne's
lace, butter-and-eggs, devil's paint-brush, chicory, meadow
sweet, evening primrose, everlasting, self-heal, Indian paint-
brush, thistles, mulleins, asters, and many more. The next group
is Wild Flowers of Woodlands and Moist Edges of Woods, which
commences with wild violets, hepatica, and spring beauty, and
then takes up Dutchman's breeches, wake robin, anemone,
columbine, jack-in-the-pulpit, lady's slipper, Indian-pipe, bunchberry, wintergreen, and others equally distinctive and full of interest. Then there is a special subdivision on Wild Flowers and
Plants of the West and South, which introduces you to the
prickly-pear cactus, rock rose, pasque flower, Spanish moss, and
others so characteristic of the regions in which they grow.

The next major division is Guide to American Trees. Here
the identifying drawing is usually a twig which gives you a close-
up of the leaves and of a cone or seed pod or berry, as it is these
which make for most rapid identification of our many beautiful
trees. We commence with the Evergreens, with their unmistakable needles—pines, larch, spruce, hemlock, fir, cedar—and the
broad-leaved holly. Then we have the Leafy Trees of the East
and North, the maple, oak, birch, beech, elm, tulip tree, sycamore, ash willow, locust, aspen, and such smaller trees as the
dogwood, shadbush, witch hazel, and mountain ash. Next we
turn to the Trees of the West and Southwest, the redwood and
sequoia, Monterey cypress, eucalyptus, cottonwood, and the
strange Joshua tree, and the amazing Giant Cactus. Then we
have Palms and Other Trees of the South, first the Live Oak, the
Pecan, and the Bald Cypress; and then the ever-entrancing palms

—the palmetto, the royal palm, the date palm, and the coconut palm.

The book concludes with a brief Guide to Minerals, Rocks, and Soils, which affords the nature lover an opportunity to identify the characteristic stones and soils which we find so closely associated with plant life, and which have such a fascination of their own that being able to recognize them really rounds out our enjoyment of the beautiful world of plants.

One special point which the author wishes to mention to all who use this book is the fact that so many of our wild flowers are known almost equally well by several different names. We have tried to include all the most common names of each. In the headings of the articles, one or another name may be singled out as the best known and the others are then mentioned within the article. For this reason, the reader is urged to use the Index at the back of the book whenever he or she is looking for a particular flower or tree or plant, as the Index, in alphabetical order, lists all the names of each, with the page reference. If you look in the Table of Contents, you will find only the name as given in the article heading; consequently we urge you to use the Index.

The author hopes that this book will add to the pleasure of your nature outings.

P. H.

Contents

WILD FLOWERS OF FIELDS, PASTURES, AND ROADSIDES, 46

WILD FLOWERS OF WOODLANDS AND MOIST EDGES OF WOODS, 77

Guide to Minerals, Rocks, and Soils, 161

GUIDE TO WILD FLOWERS AND TREES

Recognizing Wild Flowers, Trees, and Other Plant Life

Whenever you walk in the fields or woods or along a country road in spring or summer or fall, your eye catches the bright scarlet or yellow or the soft blue or pink or white of our endlessly beautiful wild flowers. Coming upon them in their natural state, you look at them with a sense of surprise, a sense quite different from that which you feel when a lovely blossom opens in a garden which you have tended carefully. The flowers of the wild are less familiar. They arouse your curiosity; you want to know something about their habits; and, above all, you want to be sure that you recognize them and can definitely name them. And this is true not only of our flowers, but equally of trees, which we include in the latter part of this book.

Along with the wild flowers in the fields and woods, you will find other forms of plant life—mosses and ferns especially—which are botanically somewhat less complex than flowers yet no less fascinating to the nature lover. We therefore commence this guide with a section called Lowly Plant Life of Fields and Woods, introducing you, with text and illustrations, to the principal common plants which are simpler than flowers; and supplementing this there is a section on Lowly Plant Life of Ponds and Streams which is brief because most of the plants of ponds are discussed in the Wild Flower section.

The book then presents a very carefully planned Guide to American Wild Flowers, which includes a wide and representative range of our choicest plants. For convenience in finding the text and illustrations, the section is subdivided into groups corresponding to the kind of location and habitat in which the flowers are most often found. These groups are: Wild Flowers of Ponds, Marshes, and Damp Meadows; Wild Flowers of Fields, Pastures, and Roadsides; Wild Flowers of Woodlands and Moist Edges of Woods; Wild Flowers and Plants of the Desert and Dry Lands.

The book then presents a Guide to American Trees, giving the reader all the information needed for ready recognition of all our principal trees, with drawings of characteristic leaves and other distinctive features. Here again the grouping is into convenient subdivisions: Evergreens; Leafy Trees of the East and North; Trees of the West and Southwest; Palms and Other Trees of the South.

The final section of the book, Guide to Minerals, Rocks, and Soils, is unique in a book on wild flowers and trees, and gives the nature lover a sense of completeness in his feeling for plant life. For here are the means of identifying common minerals and the soils which are the setting for our wild flowers; and those who are exploring for plants can with this book at the same time observe and recognize the chief minerals which they come upon in their search for our beautiful wild flowers or in studying the leaves and twigs and bark of our great trees.

Microscopic Plant Life

Before commencing our Guide, let us take a moment for

a glimpse of the very smallest forms of plant life, the single-celled green and brown Algae which are so tiny that they can only be seen under a microscope (Fig. 1). They are often found in water from a very quiet pool, yet you would not see them because they are much smaller in length and width and thickness than the width of a single human hair.

Fig. 1—Various single-celled Algae.

A vast number of these Algae close together in a pond may give the water a green or brownish cast. But you would have no way of seeing or suspecting the fascinating geometric forms of these single-celled plants until you put a drop of this water under a microscope, and looked at this hidden world.

And now that we have seen what some of these tiniest forms of plant life look like, let us turn to the varied and endlessly beautiful plants which await our eyes in the fields and woods.

Lowly Plant Life
of the Fields and Woods

The so-called lowly plants are those which do not grow
from seeds, but from tiny single cells called spores, which
are microscopic, and usually invisible unless in thick masses
or clouds, when they resemble dust. The plants of this sort
which the walker in the fields and woods is most likely to
come upon are the fungi (which include the familiar toadstools and mushrooms), the molds, the ground pines or
club-mosses, the true mosses, the lichens, and the many
varieties of ferns.

Molds. Growing all over damp decaying substances,
especially in dank, moist shady places in the woods, or in
old buildings or cellars, and especially on masses of dung in
barnyards, and so forth, one sees a very common plant and
one of the most interesting of all our lowly plants. It appears as a fleecy-white mass of very fine cobwebby threads
spreading over the surface. This is one of the so-called
Mucorales, one of the molds. Probably the one you will see
will be the common Black Mold, Bread Mold, or Dung
Mold. The scientific name of the common Dung Mold is
Mucor mucedo. Another of the very common ones is the
Black Bread Mold, or simply Bread Mold (*Rhizopus
nigricans*) (Fig. 2). Usually the searcher after these in-

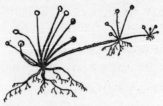

FIG. 2—Common Bread Mold.

teresting plants finds little stout dark gray stems rising thickly upwards, bearing at their tips round black button-like structures on which develop the black powder-like spores, which are like the seeds of higher plants in that they grow into new mold plants. Another similar plant, and also very common, is the so-called Fly Mold, because it is often seen growing like a round whitish halo around dead flies, particularly those which are lying in damp situations, or in water. Look at these lowly plants with a simple hand lens, or with a good reading glass if you wish to see their interesting and often beautiful structures and designs.

Toadstools and Mushrooms.   When searching for molds and other fungi, especially in the edges of woods, or in the woodlands themselves, one runs across many of the so-called toadstools. "Toadstool" is merely a popular name for what the botanists call mushrooms. Some are edible and some are poisonous. One of the common ones is the Deadly Amanita, or Death Angel, or Destroying Angel (Fig. 3), a plant which is *extremely poisonous*. Its colors vary a good deal from pure white, through pale yellows, light browns, and so on. The young plants have a globular or bell-shaped cap at first, which gradually expands or opens up (like an umbrella), and when the plant is older, or mature, its cap is nearly flat, and is apt to be somewhat moist and sticky. It may be smooth, or ornamented with little flakes and warty patches. The odor is faint and rather disagreeable, but the taste is not at all objectionable, and may be even pleasant. Be very careful of any mushroom appearing at all like the Death Angel.

FIG. 3—Deadly Amanita or Death Angel.

The collector of fungi often sees, late in the summer or early fall, graceful mushrooms usually with an urn- or dishlike cap. This may be the Urn Mushroom (*Clitocybe*) (Fig. 4). The gills (underneath) in these forms run a little

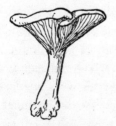

FIG. 4—Urn Mushroom.

way down the stem. The plants grow from one to six inches tall. Sometimes the cap is very deeply urn-shaped; sometimes it is only shallowly so, or even almost flat. Urn Mushrooms vary much in color. The common ones are white; others are yellowish, brown, red, and other shades. None should be eaten, for there is a poisonous species, although none are known to be fatal.

No one can walk in the woods very much without coming across the very pretty Coral Fungus (Fig. 5). Usually

FIG. 5—Coral Fungus.

this is not found growing in a single patch, but in many patches sprinkled over the forest floor. It is found especially in dampish evergreen woods, coming up through the needles of pines, spruces, hemlocks, and so on, but may occur in almost any moist low woodland. It looks very much like a bunch of coral. Its colors too are coralline, being soft ivory whites, pale straw yellows, light browns, and so forth. All the white or yellowish Coral Fungi are perfectly safe to eat, and not only safe but delicious when fried a crispy brown. But there is a pinkish, or pink-flesh-colored species, called *Clavaria dichotoma,* which is unsafe to eat. The color of this one, together with its slender, regularly branched, softish, flaccid stems, will enable the beginner to recognize it and avoid it.

Nearly everyone knows the round, white Puffballs (Fig. 6), which come up in pastures. These are all safe to eat, and

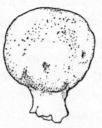

FIG. 6—Puffball.

very good indeed, sliced about an inch thick, and browned on each side in butter or bacon fat. They should be gathered when about three or four inches in diameter (before they have turned yellowish or brown in the center). No Puffballs should be eaten when small. This is to avoid mistaking them for a poisonous mushroom in its young, or button stage.

Very often in midsummer one notices a putrid, most offensive odor in the woods, or perhaps near one's summer

FIG. 7—Stink Horn.

camp or cottage, or at the edges of damp woodlands. The odor reminds one of that of a dead rat or other animal! Quite often, in the woods, this stench is given off by one of the most interesting of the fungi, the Stink Horn (Fig. 7). The whole plant, which is an erect stiff horn from three to five and one-half inches in height, grows out of a white or grayish or flesh-colored sheath, and bears at its top a cone, slightly pitted, about two inches long and half as wide. This cone, which is a sort of olive-brown color, is covered with a slimy substance which emits the fetid stench. This horrid mess is eagerly eaten by certain flies. The mucus contains the spores of the plant, and these are dispersed by the flies in this way. All the Stink Horns are regarded as poisonous.

There are thousands of species of mushrooms. Some species grow in circles which children often call "fairy rings." Mushroom study is a most interesting and beautiful one.

Mosses.   But many times as common as mushrooms are the mosses. One can hardly step out-of-doors in the country without treading on some species or other. They come up in the very cracks of the sidewalks, or between the door-steps.

All along the sides of wood roads, and in fields, pastures, even in the edges of lawns and in gardens, one finds the commonest of the large mosses, the Pigeon Wheat Moss (Fig. 8). From the top of the female plant arises the slender, yellowish, brownish, or coppery sporophyte, with a little hairy cap at its summit, which looks often like a little bird's head, bill and all. This little hairy cap gives this moss one of its common names, Hairy Cap Moss. It grows about two or three inches high, and the sporophyte is another inch or two longer. The color is a deep green, and the moss grows in great mats or carpets, or in long narrow bands

FIG. 8—Pigeon Wheat Moss.

along roadsides. Birds like to eat off the tops of this moss, the little hairy caps, which look like grains of wheat—hence the name Pigeon Wheat Moss.

The Path Moss (*Ceratodon*) (Fig. 9) is one of the most

FIG. 9—Path Moss.

commonly seen, but perhaps the most overlooked moss we have. It comes up between the bricks of a walk, even in

city and village streets, or along the edges of paths, or between stepping stones, or in stone and brick walls, and so
on. It is thick and compact, and in color a deep bluish-green
or dark green—very much like a mass of thick velvet. One
of its common names is Velvet Moss. The individual plants
of this moss are very small, roughly about a quarter of an
inch or so long. The little capsule growing out of one of
these plants is what carries the spores for reproducing the
plant. All mosses are most easily identifiable from the
shape, size, color, and markings of their little caps.

While not a common moss, the Luminous Moss (Fig. 10)

FIG. 10—Luminous Moss.

is perhaps one of our most interesting. Anyone fond of
climbing out among rocks, and exploring in little caves may
run across this lovely moss. When seen at the end of a little
cave in the rocks, it glows with a pale green flashing light
which is very beautiful indeed. This light is not given off
directly by the moss itself, but is reflected indirectly by the
leaves of the moss. However, when one sees it in the dark or
dusk of its habitat it looks for all the world as if it were
glowing with its own electric light! Look for the Luminous

Moss between the crevices of rocks, at the end of caves, and clefts, where it is dark, or at least very shady, and especially where there is dripping water or soil. Mosses make a fascinating and very beautiful study. They are easily pressed and kept in a collection. Right in your neighborhood you can probably collect and identify many different kinds.

Lichens. If you are looking for mosses, you will no doubt be gathering other plants that look much like them— the Lichens. And probably the one which will attract your notice first will be the Rosette Lichens which grow as greenish or grayish-green rosettes on tree-trunks and even more often on rocks, particularly rocks in pastures and on hillsides, and on stone walls. The very common Rosette Lichen (Fig. 11) may grow on a granite boulder in an old

FIG. 11—Rosette Lichen on boulder.

pasture. These also grow on trees, and on old boards that have lain long undisturbed in the grass, or on the sides of very old houses in the country, or on very old roofs. Lichens can be told from mosses by the fact that they have no little leaves such as a moss plant has. They are crumpled or flattish, or have little stalks, and are usually of a different sort of green from a moss—a yellowish, or grayish, or powdery green. Very often they are extremely dry, hard, or very brittle, for they dry up almost to a crisp in the hot sun, and then become very soft and green and grow when they become wet again.

On rocky cliffs, on hillsides and on mountains, one finds huge areas of the very prominent Rock Tripe Lichen (Fig. 12). These are crumpled or wrinkled saucer-shaped

FIG. 12—Rock Tripe Lichen.

lichens, dark in color (dark greenish, dark brownish, or blackish), brittle when dry, but soft, thin, and leathery when wet. They range in size from very small up to several inches in diameter. One name, *Umbilicaria*, or Umbilicus Lichen, is derived from their resemblance to an umbilicus. They are attached at the center to the rock. In northern countries these have sometimes been eaten by explorers who were hard-pressed for food. They are nutritious, but not very palatable, and make some people sick.

In old dry pastures, on hillsides, or in the edges of dry

FIG. 13—Red-capped Lichen.

woods, one sees the prettiest of the lichens, the lovely little
Red-capped Lichen (Fig. 13). The stalks of this lichen are
a soft grayish-green (bright apple-green when moist) and
the tips of many of the stalks are strikingly colored a
brilliant red. These are very common lichens, growing on
soil, and very often on old decaying stumps, and rotting logs
in the woods—not in the deep woods, but in open ones or
on their edges, where there is plenty of sunlight. Another
name for this lichen is the Scarlet-crested Lichen; still another is Matches, or British Soldiers.

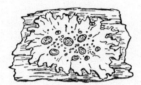

FIG. 14—Physcia, a tree-trunk lichen.

FIG. 15—Parmelia, a
common leafy lichen.

FIG. 16—Cladonia
Lichen.

Like the study of mosses, and of fungi, the study of
lichens is a very attractive one, and is followed with great
pleasure by many people. Figure 14 shows the familiar tree-
trunk lichen, Physcia. Parmelia (Fig. 15) is a common leafy
lichen, while Figure 16 shows one of the Cladonia, or cup,
lichens. Lichens are easily collected and preserved, and
may be identified by the beginner without much difficulty.

Ground Pines.   The Club Mosses (not true mosses, but

merely so-called) are much larger plants than any we have
mentioned before. They grow several inches (sometimes a
foot) high, and are known to everyone who takes rambles
in the woods. Probably the best-known one is the one which
figures so prominently in Christmas wreaths and is commonly called the Hand Lichen, or Running Pine, or Ground
Pine (*Lycopodium*) (Fig. 17). It is a lovely shining bright

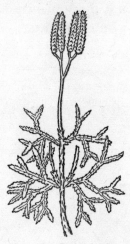

FIG. 17—Ground Pine.

green color, and spreads along the ground in woodlands, its
little green hands expanded to the light, and growing up in
long lines from a creeping stem.

Also in woodlands, and very common, too, is another of
the Ground Pines or Lycopodiums—the Club Lycopodium
or Clavate Ground Pine (Fig. 18). This is a very attractive
species, also running along the ground like the Running
Pine just described. But its branches are more erect, looking
like little green clubs, at a distance. It is more delicate than

Fig. 18—Club Moss or Clavate Ground Pine.

the Running Pine, and dries up quicker, but still is a fairly resistant, hard, shining plant, and keeps well in wreaths and decorations.

Horse-tails.   Out in the open, along roadsides, often on

Fig. 19—Scouring Rush.

the embankments of railroads, and in other dry situations, one finds very slender, pretty feathery plants which are, however, quite harsh and rigid and gritty to the touch. There are the Horse-tails, or Equisetums. A familiar one is the Scouring Rush (Fig. 19). The harsh gritty stems of this plant are gathered, tied up in firm bunches, and used to scour pots and pans. The stems contain a good deal of silica, which makes them useful in this way.

Seen especially often is the Common Horse-tail or Common Equisetum (Fig. 20). This is a more delicate species

FIG. 20—Horse-tail.

than the one described above, and is not used as a scouring plant. Some of its stalks are delicate and feathery, and some are naked and bear at their tops the little cone-like structures, pale flesh-color or brownish, in which the spores are produced—for these are still reckoned as "lowly" plants, and do not reproduce from seeds but from powdery or dust-like spores.

Ferns. Walk abroad anywhere in the country in late spring or summer, and you will find ferns everywhere—but especially in the edges of damp woodlands, along woodland roads and trails, in old pastures among the rocks, along hedgerows, in coppices, or on mountain-sides.

First let us look at a peculiar fern, one which shows that ferns may often look like other plants. It is the Adder's Tongue Fern (Fig. 21). Notice that its leaves are not cut up

FIG. 21—Adder's Tongue Fern.

into little secondary leaflets (botanists call them pinnae), but look superficially like the leaves of higher plants. Indeed this fern looks so unlike most of the ferns, that, although it is common, it is rarely noticed. It grows about four to six inches or so high, on dry grassy slopes of hillsides and along the steep grassy banks of old roads, or lower down in meadows, sometimes even in quite low swampy ground.

The searcher after plants probably runs across the Beech Ferns as often as any other ferns. One of the commonest of these is the Northern Beech Fern (Fig. 22). This lovely delicate species has a thin, slender rootstock running along on or just beneath the surface of the leafy ground and send-

FIG. 22—Northern Beech Fern.

ing up a close row of thin delicate fronds from about eight inches to a foot or so high, all covered with very fine whitish hairs and bearing small delicate brown scales on the under side along the rachis (main stem) and the main veins. The lowermost pair of leaflets are separate from those above them, and bend downward somewhat. This fern is to be looked for in low damp woodlands, wet thickets, and moist crevices among rocks and cliffs. Its range extends from our northern states southward along the mountains, and it is most always found, no matter where it grows, in cool situations.

But probably the most common fern of all on rocks and cliffs is the Rock Polypody (Fig. 23). This is also called the Rockfern, and the Rockcap Fern. The rootstock is thick

FIG. 23—Rock Polypody or Rockfern.

and stout, and covered densely with brown scales. From it arise rows of evergreen fronds, oblong in shape and from six to about eight inches or so in length, rich green, sometimes light, sometimes dark. These ferns are always seen by those who ramble among the rocky hills and mountains, where the lovely fronds grow thickly, covering dry rocks, or capping large glacial boulders, or sometimes growing along cliffs, and in cracks in high ledges of rock. Sometimes it is found covering talus slopes, or less often on wooded banks or running over fallen tree-trunks. One has no trouble in identifying this fern because of its love for rocks, but if one gathers many specimens from various localities, one soon notices that their fronds differ in form. At least ten different varieties of the Rock Polypody have received names.

Another very common woodland fern, not growing on rocks, however, is the Christmas Fern (Fig. 24). This fern

FIG. 24—Christmas Fern.

is a large one; its fronds are seen growing in bunches, and reaching out to a length of one foot to two feet, the young plants being shorter, of course, and more delicate. The rootstock from which these fronds arise is very stout and chaffy, and the stems of the fronds are very scaly. In color this fern is a rich green; those growing in deep woods are a dark color, while those growing where there is more light, are apt to be lighter in color. All these plants are evergreen, however; the fronds do not wither in the fall. For this reason one can find perfectly good green fronds in winter—hence the name Christmas Fern. This fern is very adaptable as to the soil it grows on, being found in all kinds of woodlands, wooded slopes of hills and on mountainsides, in the humus-filled crevices in the rocks, on hummocks in swampy lands, and often in open thickets. It can be transplanted from its woodland habitat, and thrives well in gardens and along the walls of houses.

Very often when you are loitering along some wooded roadway bordered with little rocky cuts, or climbing around on a rocky hillside, or on some wooded slope, you will run across a little plant with long narrow leaves that seem to be looping their way along the ground like strawberry runners, rooting at their tips and then sending up another

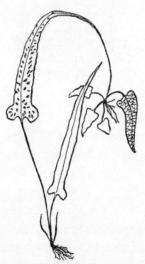

FIG. 25—Walking Fern.

little plant from these tips. This habit makes this particular fern easily recognizable. It is the celebrated Walking Fern (Fig. 25), said to be rare, but, like so many things said to be rare, is not very rare to those who search for it. You will find it growing on sheltered ledges, and along cliffs, and on talus slopes, as well as in the places mentioned above. Sometimes it occurs on hummocks of humus in damp woodlands, in swampy low spots, and sometimes on tree-trunks. But most commonly of all you will find it on limestone rocks, where it sometimes grows in such masses that from a distance the masses resemble mats of coarse grass. This little fern thrives well in dish gardens and in terrariums (the so-called ferneries). From one fern plant there will arise as many little daughter-plants as there are fronds to the parent, each frond bending down to root at its tip and start a new

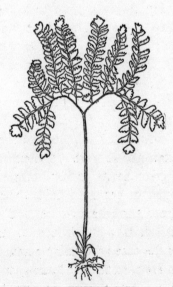

FIG. 26—Maidenhair Fern.

little plant. Thus the plant "walks" along, spreading outward from a center.

Still keeping to the wooded slopes where you have found
the Walking Fern, continue your search for the lovely
Maidenhair Fern (Fig. 26), which often goes under the
name of Northern Maidenhair. The fronds of this fern are
quite different from any other divided-frond fern, and you
will have no difficulty in identifying it. The stems are shining blackish-brown—like thin stalks of polished mahogany,
and the little leaflets (pinnae) are heavily edged with the
spore-bearing structures, giving them a very unusual decorative appearance. This lovely delicate fern grows to a
height of a few inches to almost two feet tall. The fronds
arise from slender running rootstocks, which may be transplanted into gardens, where they thrive readily.

Of all the ferns you will find on your walks afield, the
Climbing Fern (Fig. 27) will prove to be the most unique.
It is our only fern which climbs with a vine-like habit of
growth. Look for this in wet mossy thickets, or in very open
moist woodlands, where there are plenty of shrubs and tall
weedy growths, or along springy banks. For this fern,
rising like all ferns from a running slender rootstock, sends
up long scattering fronds, their very slender vine-like stems
twining around shrubs and tall weeds (often such plants
as goldenrod, aster, and so forth), and exposing their little
leaflets like tiny green hands prettily outspread. This pretty
fern is often found in hot open fields, twining about the
stems of goldenrods and meadowsweet and even about the
stems of stout tall grasses. But it likes to "keep its feet in
the water," as is the case with many plants. The spores of
this unusual fern are born on little leaflets, at the ends of the
stems, where there are clusters of tiny little hand-like

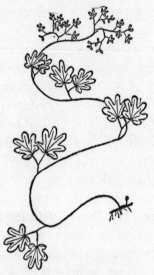

FIG. 27—Climbing Fern.

growths. This Climbing Fern is a rather rare fern, although when you find it, you will probably find many plants growing closely associated with it. Preserve it carefully, for it is likely to be exterminated.

Lowly Plant Life of Ponds and Streams

We take up here two lowly forms of plant life found in the smaller fresh water bodies. The other familiar plants of ponds and streams are wild flowers, which we include in their location group in the Guide to American Wild Flowers which follows.

Spirogyra. Often on bright sunny days in late spring and summer the walker's eye is attracted to vivid bright green growths in the clear waters of a brook. The appearance is that of long streams of waving green hair, swinging back and forth in the current of the stream where the flow is not too rapid. If a stick or the hand is dipped into the mass it is felt to be rather slimy and stringy. Pick up a bit of this slimy green string, and look at it under a microscope. It will then be seen to consist of delicate green threads. The plant itself is called Spirogyra (Fig. 28). It is one of the green algae, very lowly plants, and consists of cells strung one along the other like the cars in a train. Each cell contains a pretty, flat, twisted green body, the chloroplast, which gives the green color to the plant. There are many of these bright green, thread-like (filamentous) algae growing in the water. (We have shown some still simpler algae, consisting of single cells, in Fig. 1, page 3). The Spirogyra

FIG. 28—Spirogyra or Pond Scum; *above,* as it appears in the water; *below,* as seen under a microscope.

may be identified by the way in which its masses string out into a single point, when lifted from the water, and send off drop after drop from the point, as if it were greased. Spirogyra grows not only in streams, but also along the borders of lakes and pools, where the water is pure. Often the masses will give off oxygen bubbles, which buoy them up in the water. In this condition the green masses appear rather frothy; hence they are often called Frog Spittle, although of course there is no connection with the activity of frogs. Probably the name under which they are familiar to most of us is Pond Scum.

Nitella.   A plant often found by those who poke about in sluggish streams or in shallow pools is Nitella, or Stonewort (Fig. 29). This plant is a bright green (or when covered with sediment is a grayish-green), with pretty, deli-

FIG. 29—Nitella or Stonewort.

cate whorls of what appear to be leaves. These leaf-like structures are only stems, for the plant is a lowly algal plant, and lacks leaves entirely. It is often harsh and gritty and stiff to the touch because of a deposit of lime made by the plant cells; hence the name, Stonewort. Nitella (and Chara, a very similar but stouter plant) grow in all sorts of fresh waters where there is very little or no current. However, they definitely seem to prefer fresh water and are very seldom found where the water is brackish.

Guide to American Wild Flowers

Of all forms of plant life, the nature lover finds greatest variety and endless fascination in wild flowers, which provide such abundant brilliance of color during their season of bloom, and which earlier are of interest for the distinctive shape and texture and shading of their leaves, and later for their seed pods and other autumn signs of a new spring to come.

We have grouped the wild flowers according to the location in which they are most often found. We begin with the flowers of ponds, marshes, and wet meadows; next we take up those of the fields and pastures and roadsides; then those seen in the woods and at the moist edges of woods; and finally we take up the flowers which are found chiefly in the western and southern parts of the country.

WILD FLOWERS OF PONDS, MARSHES, AND DAMP MEADOWS

Pond Lily. In still waters everywhere, especially along the shallow margins of ponds and sluggish streams, one sees the round, bud-like Yellow Pond Lily, or Horse Lily (Fig. 30). This is the common odorless yellow lily often found together with the widely open fragrant Pond Lily. Its leaves float out broadly ovate in form on the surface of the water,

Fig. 30—Yellow Pond Lily or Horse Lily.

and its yellow flowers show six greenish sepals which are sometimes tinged with purple. Inside may be seen a pale ruddy or deep golden-yellow disc, which is the stigma. This flower never opens very widely, as do the other water lilies.

Pickerelweed.   In summer, say from June through September, you may notice a blue haze appearing along the muddy margins of ponds and languid streams. This is caused by the blooming of masses of Pickerelweed (Fig. 31). The stems of this plant rise up to a height of about one to three feet, bearing at their tops dense four-inch-long spikes of bright violet-blue flowers. Each flower shows two

Fig. 31—Pickerelweed.

yellow spots on its upper lip. The leaves of the plant are thick, smooth, and dark green. These Pickerelweed plants, thickly massed together, furnish abundant food for deer and moose; and below the waterline they offer a harborage for many species of fish, among them the popular game fishes: pike and pickerel—hence the name of the plant. But the plant might just as appropriately be named Deerweed, or Mooseweed. It grows from Prince Edward Island south to Florida and west to Ontario, Minnesota, and Oklahoma. Another species, with slenderer leaves, is found from Delaware to Florida and Texas.

Arrowheads. The lovely little Arrowheads (Fig. 32) are white-flowered water plants, growing thickly in the edge

FIG. 32—Arrowhead.

of the water, or wherever it is shallow. The leaves are a deep lustrous green, and look like arrowheads, either fat or narrow, according to the species, of which there are a dozen or so that are fairly common. Their pollen is thick and yellow, and is distributed by a variety of carriers, among which are the large, delicate, glassy-winged dragonflies, which one sees always glancing about in the air in situations where the arrowheads grow. Arrowheads are often dug up and transplanted in water gardens and garden pools; they are prized because of the beauty of the shining green, prettily-shaped leaves as much as for their blossoms.

Wild Iris.   In damp meadows, and marshes, the Blue Flag (Fig. 33) or Wild Iris is a common and well-known flower. It is a tall, handsome, decorative plant, with straight,

FIG. 33—Blue Flag or Wild Iris.

light green, flat leaves, and violet-blue flowers, prettily veined, often with deep violet over a whitish ground. The base is usually tinted with yellow. The name, Iris, is from the Greek, meaning "rainbow," and refers to the prismatic colors of the flower.

Skunk Cabbage.   Perhaps the most interesting of all the early spring flowers, and certainly the very first one to blossom after Christmas, is the humble little Skunk Cabbage (Fig. 34). This pokes its way up through the cold muddy ground, as a sort of fat spike. This is the blossom-hood, or spathe, as it is called, a thick coiled overcoat, of a very attractive color, being madder-purple, brownish, or greenish, streaked with these same colors. Inside it may be a dark reddish. Within this spathe is a stout, club-shaped organ known as the spadix. Tear open the spathe and you will expose this part of the flower. In reality, while we call the whole thing the Skunk-Cabbage "flower," the Skunk Cabbage is really a whole bouquet of flowers. These are compactly set on the spadix, or club, within; they are small, and each one is perfect (that is, bears stamens and a pistil). These plants give off a fetid or skunk-like odor (or the odor of very strong garlic), which attracts numerous insects to

FIG. 34—Skunk Cabbage.

the inside of the spathe, where they help fertilize the flowers. In spite of the somewhat objectionable odor of the plant, it is hailed with joy by all those who love the woods, for it is the very first herald of spring. One of its names is Spring Welcome, a very pretty and appropriate name. It is interesting to remember, when you see the lowly Skunk Cabbage poking its sharp spathe up through the frozen mud of January or February, that this plant is a very close relative of the pure and spotless white Calla Lily, the purple-mottled spathe of the cabbage being the homologue of the snowy petal-like spathe of the lily. It is also the homologue of the "pulpit" part of the Jack-in-the-Pulpit "flower."

Marsh Marigold, King-Cup, or "Cowslip."   From April to June, Marsh Marigolds (Fig. 35) may be found in flower in swamps, wet meadows, and along the margins of small streams. The plants are often gathered for spring greens, and the buds are pickled as a substitute for capers. This lovely species is one of our vanishing plants, and hence should be gathered only when it is very abundant. The

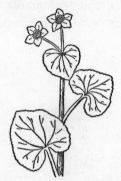

FIG. 35—Marsh Marigold.

flowers, from one to one-and-a-half inches across, bear from five to nine deep golden-yellow, petal-like sepals; petals are absent. The leaves are a shining deep green, and the smooth succulent stem is hollow. Marsh Marigolds grow from Labrador to Newfoundland and south to South Carolina; and westward to Tennessee, Nebraska, and on to Alaska.

Cat-Tail, Cat-o-Nine-Tails, or Reed-Mace.   Cat-Tails (Fig. 36) are in their best full flower in the early summer months. There are no showy petals to be seen, but flowers of two kinds appear on a long dense cylindrical spike about an inch in diameter. The upper part of the spike bears long hairs and yellowish stamens which shower their powdery

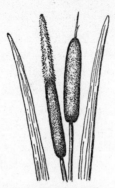

FIG. 36—Cat-Tail.

pollen down upon the female flowers beneath. The lower part of the spike is the brown compact part bearing the brown female flowers and bristles, which later become downy and buoy up and away on the breeze the minute nutlets. The plants grow up to a height of from four to eight feet, and are found in marshes and shallow water from New-foundland and Alaska south throughout most of the United States and Mexico. There is a slenderer species of Cat-Tail, called the Narrow-Leaved Cat-Tail, in which the male and female flowers are widely separated on the same stalk.

Swamp Rose-Mallow or Mallow-Rose.   The large, showy, hollyhock-like flowers of the Mallow-Rose (Fig. 37) come into bloom in the late summer months. They are from four to seven inches across, pink or white in color, and usually deep crimson at the bases of the petals. The plants themselves are shrub-like, and rise up to a height of from four to seven feet. This species, like other mallows, gives off a somewhat unpleasant musky or mousey odor. Among the several species of mallows occurs one of espe-cially great interest, namely the familiar and infinitely valu-able Cotton plant of our South. The Mallow-Rose or Swamp

FIG. 37—Swamp Rose-Mallow.

Rose-Mallow is ordinarily found near the coast in brackish waters from Massachusetts south to Florida and inland in the vicinity of salt springs.

Ironweed.   In the late summer many low moist areas are gay and abloom with the deep purple or violet Ironweed (Fig. 38), the dull magenta Joe-Pye-weed, and the dull white Boneset. All these stout tall plants bear flat-topped

FIG. 38—Ironweed.

clusters of flowers. Each flower-head is made up of multitudes of minute florets. Tea made of the Joe-Pye-weed was early used to cure fevers; and tea made of Boneset was used both as a bitter tonic and for relief from colds. These teas are still made and used in many country districts. Several species of Ironweed are found in the United States and Canada. The plants are widely distributed from Ontario south to Mississippi and west to Manitoba, Oklahoma, and Texas.

Jewelweed.   A quite different plant, with showy, lovely pale yellow flowers, massed thickly along shaded streams and damp roadsides, is the Jewelweed, or Touch-me-not (Fig. 39). These plants grow up very tall and rank, and are profusely hung with their yellow blossoms. Sometimes these blossoms are of an orange hue, sometimes spotted or

FIG. 39—Jewelweed.

freckled all over with reddish brown. The name "Touch-me-not" refers to the action of the little ripened seed-pods. In late summer and early fall when these are mature they look like little green bananas. Touch one on its end, and instantly it snaps into several thin coiled parts, with explosive violence, hurling the little seeds in all directions. Thus is the plant disseminated. In some country districts the plant is called Silver Leaf. Immerse one of the leaves in water, and you will see why this name is a very happy one. There are two kinds of Touch-me-nots, the Pale or Pallid species, and the Spotted species. In one the flowers incline to a darker orange color; in the other they are a pallid but clear yellow.

Spiderwort.   In very rich, black, or moist ground grows the Spiderwort (Fig. 40). The delicate flowers are a light violet-blue, and like those of the Dayflower, to which they

FIG. 40—Spiderwort.

are very closely related, they are very perishable, lasting only a very few hours. The stems are very mucilaginous as you will find if you pick them, and grow up to a height of one to one and a half feet. The genus to which this plant belongs has the interesting name of Tradescantia, named for John Tradescant, who was royal gardener to Charles I of England. The early spring queen bumblebees love the flowers of this plant, and eagerly search it out because of its wealth of pollen, stumbling clumsily about among the stamens and becoming covered with the yellow fertilizing dust which they carry to another flower and rub off on the stigma. This flower is a familiar, old-fashioned garden flower, common around many farm houses in the east and north.

Sundews.   All along the damp banks of some country

road, as well as in damp hillside meadows and pastures, or in low swampy ground on the hummocks, you will often find the ground carpeted with a mat of plants of the sundews. The Round-leaved Sundew (Fig. 41) is the one that you will probably most often see. The little flower-stalk is only a few inches high. The funny little leaves, lying spread

FIG. 41—Round-leaved Sundew.

out around the plant almost flat on the ground as a sort of rosette, are rounded, and thickly beset with reddish, gland-bearing bristles. When the sun shines on the leaves they appear as if covered with tiny sparkling dew-drops. These tiny droplets are a gluey secretion by means of which insects are entrapped and glued fast. The little reddish bristles then close over the insect, and the leaves absorb and feed upon the body juices. The plant is reddish in color, and is so saturated with color that if pressed between pieces of paper it stains them a deep madder-purple. Sundews grow well in a saucer of moss indoors, where they make interesting little plant pets. Plant some in this way, and then feed the leaves with flies, mosquitoes, or even tiny fragments of meat.

Buttercups.   In the spring all lovers of the country look with eagerness for the appearance of the buttercups. There are many of these delightful golden yellow, cheerful flowers; the commonest of them, and the best-loved one, is the Swamp or Meadow Buttercup (Fig. 42). This species is

FIG. 42—Swamp or Meadow Buttercup.

confined to low, wet meadows and swampy places. The flowers are a deep butter yellow, and are an inch or so in diameter. The stout hollow stem is smooth, but sometimes one is found covered with very fine hairs. Like most of the other members of its group, this pretty spring blossom is dependent chiefly on the little beelike flies, Bombylius, and the tiny bees of the family Andrenidae, for fertilization. The minute creatures can be seen about the blossoms on a damp, warm summer's day, flying swiftly here and there, or crawling about among the delicate stamens. This buttercup is not the first buttercup of the spring. The first one to appear is a somewhat similar species, the Early Buttercup, which is a woodland or hillside dweller. This plant is rather lower in growth habit than the Swamp Buttercup, with fine silky hairs on its stems and leaves.

Meadow Rues. Another damp or swampy-ground, showy flower is the Meadow Rue. There are several species of this plant. The Tall Meadow Rue (Fig. 43) is a foamy white flower borne on a tall, almost bush-like plant rising

FIG. 43—Meadow Rue.

up from three to sometimes ten feet in height! Not often do we find it so tall, however. Its crown of flowers on a warm spring day is surrounded by numerous bees, moths, and the smaller butterflies, by which it is fertilized. The flowers give off a delicate sweet fragrance, somewhat grassy, but very pleasant; for human nostrils it does not, however, carry far, although no doubt for insects the odor is quite a powerful lure for a long distance. This large showy plant is most often found where a sluggish stream meanders its way through a low field, or along a damp country road, where the delicate foamy-white or greenish-white blossoms rise up over the tops of the ferns like soft round clouds or balls of mist.

Blue-eyed Grass. Down close to the ground, in damp situations, one sees beautiful little deep violet-blue six-pointed stars, with white and yellow centers, nestling tightly among the grasses, whole clusters of them together. These are the flowers of the Blue-eyed Grass (Fig. 44). The plant itself is stiff and grass-like, its leaves pale blue-green, very narrow, and poked upright like the grass leaves with which they are surrounded. If you pick these lovely little flowers you will soon suffer a disappointment, for they close up tightly very soon. Left to itself in the moist coolness where

FIG. 44—Blue-eyed Grass.

it belongs, it keeps its little blue eyes wide open (one of its names is Eye Bright) until the sun is high, and shines directly on it. When this happens, and the grass all around becomes hot and dry, the little blue eyes close up.

Star of Bethlehem.   Quite like the Blue-eyed Grass in its choice of habitat, and in its manner of growth, too, is the grass-like Star of Bethlehem (Fig. 45). The dark green leaves are narrow, and the pretty flowers are white inside and green-lined outside. But unlike the Blue-eye, the little Star of Bethlehem, or White-eye, opens only in the sunshine. Its scientific name is Ornithogalum, meaning "bird's milk," and refers to the egg-white color of the inside of the

FIG. 45—Star of Bethlehem.

blossom. This species is an ornamental plant, imported from Europe, and escaped from our gardens.

Fringed Gentian. In late September the walker in the woods and fields comes upon the heavenly blue Fringed Gentian (Fig. 46) with a start of surprise and joy. It surely is one of the treasures of our countryside. Many poets have sung its praises, and many painters have immortalized it also on their canvases. The plant grows in damp situations, reaching a height of one to two feet. The flowers are borne

FIG. 46—Fringed Gentian.

either singly in a plant, or in clusters of from two or three
to many. Since it is biennial, with seeds that are easily
washed away, we may not always find it in the same place
year after year, as we do so many plants. This gives it all
the charm of uncertainty and mystery. Look for this along
brooks, in low damp fields, in wet pastures overgrown with
grass tufts and small bushes, on the edge of moist woodlands, or along the damp and ditchy borders of country
roads and lanes. But pick it sparingly, leaving most of the
flowers you find to set their seeds, and carry back with you
only one or two perfect blossoms. The flowers that bloom
in the shade are a lovely pale, heavenly blue; but those in
the bright sun are apt to be a deep full azure blue—like the
color of the sky seen from the top of a lofty mountain—
almost a "black" blue sometimes. In a late season, one finds
straggling plants blooming in November, even December.

WILD FLOWERS OF FIELDS, PASTURES, AND ROADSIDES

Clovers.   In our lawns and along roadsides one sees the
little white clovers so commonly that one scarcely gives
them much attention. The Alsike (Fig. 47), or common
White Clover, as it is inaccurately called, has a branching,

FIG. 47—Alsike Clover.

stout, and rather juicy stem. The pretty little blossoms are usually white, but vary from this color through cream color, or creamy pink, to crimson pink. But the chief color is white. This clover is sweet-scented, and rich in nectar. The withered florets become brownish and turn downward. The plants, if left alone and not mowed off, may grow from one to two feet high. The White Clover, another species (the Alsike should not be called by this name), is also one of our most common clovers, found along grassy country roads. Its leaves are rounder than those of the Alsike Clover, and there are sometimes four or five leaflets on a single stalk. The blossoms are not so apt to be pink as are those of the Alsike, but are mostly white, creamy, or at most flesh-color. This plant is said to be the same as the Shamrock of Ireland. It grows from four or five to ten inches or so long, and creeps by runners. It is common everywhere in the northern regions, even the extreme north.

White Daisy or Ox-Eye Daisy. Perhaps the most familiar of our wild flowers is this daisy which whitens the fields and roadsides chiefly in May and June, and which continues to flower less abundantly into November. The flower-heads, from one to two inches across, are composed of miniature perfect yellow disc florets, and showy white female ray florets. The plants are straight and erect, and rise up to a height of from one to three feet. They are looked upon as a pest by the farmer, who calls them Whiteweed, or Farmer's Curse. To children they are a favorite in fortune-telling. As each white ray-floret is pulled off, the children chant: "He loves me, he loves me not." The White Daisy (Fig. 48), originally a native in Asia, was naturalized in Europe and then in North America, and is now found abundantly from Newfoundland and Quebec south to New

FIG. 48—White Daisy.

York and New Jersey; and less commonly (or sometimes absent) southward and westward.

Black-Eyed Susan or Yellow Daisy.   In mid-summer many dry fields and sandy barren places become golden with these beautiful daisies, which have the picturesque

FIG. 49—Black-Eyed Susan.

name Black-Eyed Susan (Fig. 49). Their heads, from two to four inches across, bear showy deep orange-colored rays and a dull brownish or purplish cone in the center, which

makes children sometimes call them "chocolate-drop
daisies." The tough rigid stems (from one to two feet
high) and also the deep olive-green leaves are rough and
bristly. The Black-Eyed Susan is an aggressive perennial
weed which originated in our western plains but is now ex-
tending its range rapidly eastward. It makes itself at home
in dry fields and barrens all the way from Maine southward
to Florida and west to Manitoba, Colorado, and Texas.

Queen Anne's Lace.   The Wild Carrot, or Queen Anne's
Lace, or Bird's Nest (Fig. 50) is really a lovely flower.

FIG. 50—Queen Anne's Lace or Wild Carrot.

How often do we pass it by because it is so common. It
was introduced from Europe (as so many of our wild flowers were), and now has taken possession of our fields. In
a cultivated garden it is a noxious weed; hence, one of its
names is Devil's Plague. Although it is said to be the pro-
genitor of the cultivated carrot, its long tapering root is not
at all like the sweet agreeable carrot root. It is stringy and
harsh, acrid to the taste, and is reputed to be actually poisonous. The first season, a crown of leaves is produced; the
flowers follow the second season, and rise up on long rigid

stalks to a height of two to three feet. Wild carrot flowers are very desirable in bouquets, where their lacy white texture shows to advantage. Their leaves, too, are decorative, being finely cut and divided.

Butter-and-Eggs or Toad-Flax. Toad-Flax blossoms abundantly all summer long from May to October, displaying its bright yellow flowers with their deep golden-orange palates, from one to one and a quarter inches in length (Fig. 51). The pale, smooth stems rise up to a height of

FIG. 51—Butter-and-Eggs.

from one to three feet. The blossoms are somewhat like a small yellow snapdragon. The leaves as well as the stems are pale green and smooth. The Butter-and-Eggs or Toad-Flax is a European plant, naturalized in North America, and may be found growing in dry fields, waste places, and along roadsides, from Newfoundland south to Georgia and west to Manitoba, Oregon, and New Mexico.

Orange Hawkweed, Tawny Hawkweed, or Devil's Paint-Brush. From June to October, fields, clearings, and waste places are often aflame with the brilliant orange-tawny flowers of this common hawkweed (Fig. 52). The fragrant flower-heads are two-thirds to one inch across. The coarse

FIG. 52—Orange Hawkweed.

leaves, from two to five inches long, and the slender stalks, from six to eighteen inches high, are bristly throughout with short stiff black hairs. Because of this feature the plant is often called Grim-the-Collier. This rapidly-spreading weed scatters its seeds as does the dandelion, and also spreads by means of rooting stolons which form dense mats of numerous rosettes. The Orange Hawkweed is comparatively a newcomer from Europe, but already extends from Newfoundland south to Virginia, and west to Ontario, Indiana, and Iowa. Also known as Devil's Paint-Brush.

Chicory, Succory, or Blue Sailors. Throughout the entire summer this beautiful weed flowers profusely in fields

FIG. 53—Chicory.

and along roadsides. In the early part of each day the flower of Chicory (Fig. 53) is a pretty, pale blue, but as the day advances the color changes to violet-blue, and finally alters to a faded gray. One sometimes, but not often, finds a plant which bears pink, or white, flowers. Chicory flowers do not open on cloudy days. The plants, rising up to a height of from one to three feet, have stiff, tough stems. The large roots, roasted and ground, are used as a substitute for coffee, or as an adulterative to it. The plant, originally a native of the Old World, now may be found in this country from Newfoundland south to North Carolina and west to Washington and California.

Sweet Clover or Melilot.   As the illustration shows, the Sweet Clovers (Fig. 54) are very different both in blossom and stem from the common Clovers which we have already

Fig. 54—Sweet Clover or Melilot.

discussed. The flowers of these herbaceous plants perfume the roadsides from the very early summer, and continue to bloom less abundantly throughout the summer months. The entire plant becomes so fragrant upon drying that it is often laid among linens to impart to them its own pleasant odor.

The commonest of all the sweet clovers are the White Sweet Clover and the Yellow Sweet Clover. These plants usually bear one-sided flower clusters from two to four inches in length. The stems are very slender. Plants of the White Sweet Clover often attain a height of ten feet; plants of the Yellow Sweet Clover somewhat less than this. These Melilots, of which there are four species, have made themselves very much at home nearly everywhere throughout most of North America except in the extreme north.

Meadow Sweet.   Hillside pastures are the favorite resorts of the lovely delicate Meadow Sweet (Fig. 55). The flowers are white or sometimes a very pale creamy pink,

Fig. 55—Meadow Sweet.

and are not fragrant, in spite of the name. You will recognize this plant from its tall stems, rather woody, covered with thin alternate leaves right up to the flower spike. The leaves are coarsely toothed. At a distance the whole plant looks like a bouquet of stiffish stems, crowned by the white fluffy flowers. Sometimes whole hillsides are covered with these pretty, bushy plants. Another plant, as common as, and sometimes commoner than, the Meadow Sweet, and looking much like it in general growth habit, is the Hard-hack or Steeple Bush. This plant bears a longish, conical spike of flowers at the top of its stems. The flowers are usu-ally a lovely deep rose-pink. This, and the Meadow Sweet, are the two prettiest of our bushy pasture-flowers.

Wild Strawberries.   All walkers and searchers in the country know the Wild Strawberry (Fig. 56). There are two familiar species of wild strawberry: the common one is

Fig. 56—Wild Strawberry.

called simply Wild Strawberry, and the other one is the American Wood Strawberry, a slenderer form with thinner leaflets which are more ovate and less wedge-shaped than those of the Wild Strawberry. Moreover, their undersides are clothed with silvery silky hairs. The scarlet fruit is also more conical, and the seeds appear, not in little pits on the fruit, but upon the shining surface. The Wood Strawberry is noteworthy for its very long, delicate runners. The Wild Strawberry is sometimes called the Wild Virginia Straw-berry. Sometimes the cultivated strawberry escapes from gardens, and may be found nearby along roadsides and paths.

Wild Roses.   There are several kinds of wild roses. A common form (Fig. 57) has petals which are a lovely pink, or sometimes deeper crimson-pink, or sometimes a pale shell-pink—its color variations are many. But however it is colored, it is always a simple, delicate, seemingly fragile flower—so much lovelier than many of our large, heavy, cabbagy garden varieties. The showy, globular red fruits, or "rose-hips," resemble little red apples (in fact the rose and the apple belong to the same family, Rosaceae). They

FIG. 57—Wild Rose.

are sour, but of good flavor, and are used in making jams and jellies. They are said to be especially rich in vitamins. Some of the Wild Roses native to America are the Smooth Rose, Swamp Rose, Dwarf Wild Rose, Pasture Rose, Northeastern Rose, and the lovely little Sweetbrier, Wild Rose, or Eglantine. This is the Eglantine of the English poets, and the rose itself is adventive from Europe. It is remarkable for its sweet-scented foliage, unlike our Wild Roses of America, and to most nostrils is reminiscent of wild apples. Its stems are long, slender, and beautiful with their compactly set clusters of small pink roses. Sometimes the blooms are whitish, creamy, or pale creamy-pink, rarely deep pink. This lovely wild rose is now well established and common along old stone walls, roadsides, and pastures, from Tennessee and Virginia, northward. Another European species, occurring along with the Eglantine, though not nearly so abundantly, is the Dog Rose. This bears simply toothed leaves, which are not nearly so fragrant.

Evening Primrose.   The lovely Evening Primrose (Fig. 58) has tall stalks which rise up to a height of one to six feet (although not very commonly so tall, it is true), displaying the pretty, large, bright yellow flowers. The leaves

FIG. 58—Evening Primrose.

are a light green color and the yellow flowers are slightly lemon-scented, with prominent spreading stamens. The blossoms open in the very late afternoon, just before sundown, or if the day is very dark and cloudy, sometimes quite early in the afternoon, and fade in the strong sunlight of the following day. At the falling twilight the flowers unfold their petals swiftly; often they burst open with a sudden pop. To watch an Evening Primrose opening is an event which no one should miss. The sweet odors that pour out from this newly opened chalice attract night-flying moths, which fertilize the flowers. Evening Primroses inhabit all sorts of dry soils. Look for them in old fields, meadows, along roadsides and country lanes, in abandoned gardens, and in all sorts of waste places. The tall stalks and yellow flowers make them easy to find. Many people dig them up and transplant them in their gardens, or plant the seeds—such interesting and decorative plants are they, and so very fragrant in an evening garden. (See also White-flowered Evening Primrose.)

Evening Lychnis.   What unusual flowers does the Evening Lychnis (Fig. 59) bear! You cannot mistake it. This charming plant was imported from the Old Country, and now flourishes in all sorts of waste places and the borders of roadways, paths, and fields, all over the eastern portion of the United States. The Evening Lychnis, as its name implies, is chiefly an evening blossom; that is, it opens at this time. In the bright light of a sunny morning you will find the blossoms tightly closed. The flowers are very fragrant. Their chief peculiarity, and the feature which enables you to identify the plant with certainty, is the much inflated

Fig. 59—Evening Lychnis.

calyx, looking like a long balloon. Along its ribs there run maroon or crimson lines, which are somewhat hairy and sticky. Later on this becomes still more inflated and rounder, and then withers away, leaving exposed the vase-shaped light brownish seed-vessel. The Evening Lychnis grows to a height of about one to two feet, and blossoms all summer long, from late June or early July into October. Even in November one may find plants still in bloom in sheltered spots. Somewhat similar, but with much rounder balloons beneath the petals, is the Bladder Campion. This is a foreign species, now perfectly naturalized in America. The balloons beneath the petals are much different in color from those of the Evening Lychnis; they are a lovely delicate pale green, beautifully veined with darker green, in appearance reminding one of small citron melons. This plant grows commonly in moist low places along roadsides and country paths, and in all sorts of moist hollows and meadows. Another one, somewhat similar, is the Sleepy Catchfly, whose very small flowers expand their petals only for short periods of time when the sun is shining on them. The name Catchfly is given to the plant because the joints of its stem are very glutinous. This prevents the ascent of ants and other creeping insects which would steal the nectar of the flower, and which are useless to the plant as carriers of pollen. The balloon-like calyx is crowned at its tip with very small insignificant pinkish petals. This feature forms the identification character for the species. In the Starry Campion the petals of the flower are star-shaped, with much-fringed edges—unlike the others.

Chickweed.   Who does not know the little Chickweed (Fig. 60)—the commonest weed of all Europe, and almost the commonest American weed as well? It is a weak-stemmed little annual plant. Its little white star-flowers bear sepals which are green, and much larger than the petals. It grows all over bare places, and along walks, and in drive-

FIG. 60—Chickweed.

ways, everywhere dotting the ground and grass with its pretty little stars, so often overlooked. It is especially fond of damp ground, where it runs rank, and forms mats. The plants themselves may grow from two to four inches high. Chickweeds are much relished as food by chickens, and also by wild birds, especially those of the Sparrow or Finch family. Thrushes and other ground-dwelling birds are also fond of it.

Pigweed.   In cultivated ground and in gardens, as well as along roads, one finds the tall robust Pigweed (Fig. 61). The stems and leaves are a light green, and are roughish in

FIG. 61—Pigweed.

texture, and the dull green flowers are borne on a stiff bristly spike. This plant is reckoned an annoying weed. It was imported from Europe, and grows from one to seven feet or so in height. The seeds of this surprising weed have been known to survive in the soil for more than thirty years, which accounts for the persistence of the plant in all cultivated ground. It is also known by the names of Redroot Pigweed and Chinaman's Greens, although its palatability is questionable. Still, it is eaten, and if gathered when very young in the early spring, certainly adds to the wholesome green vegetable food-supply of those who live in the country.

Lady's Thumb.   In damp waste places, or sometimes in dry situations, invading the garden, and running around

FIG. 62—Lady's Thumb.

among all sorts of crops, one finds the extremely common Lady's Thumb (Fig. 62). Its pretty crimson-pink flowers are much admired in small bouquets. The stems grow from six inches to two feet tall: they are smooth, and often reddish or purplish at their bases. The leaves are pointed at both ends, and bear a brownish spot near their centers. This is said to be the mark made by the thumb of St. Mary who once pinched the plant which she was gathering to make a poultice for St. Joseph, who had hurt his hand in his carpenter's shop. Hence the name Our Lady's Thumb, now shortened to Lady's Thumb. These thumb-marked leaves, and the pretty pink flowers will identify the plant for you. There are several kinds of these plants, all somewhat similar, and all named Polygonum. Other names for them are Smartweeds, Knotweeds, and Heartweed. One species has long climbing stems armed with small numerous backward-pointing prickles. This is known as a Tearthumb. But it is a Polygonum like the rest. It is extremely common. Its leaves are arrowhead-shaped, and hence it is called the Arrow-leaved Tearthumb. Another one looks like Buckwheat, and is perfectly smooth, with a slender, climbing, reddish stem, and arrowhead-shaped leaves. Its flowers range from greenish white to pale magenta. Look for these interesting Polygonums—they are very common, and you will be sure to find several growing within a small area.

Mustards. Beside roads, and in grain fields, and in all cultivated land, in fact, one sees the very common, bright yellow flowers of the various mustards. One of these is

Fig. 63—Black Mustard.

called the Black Mustard (Fig. 63). These plants are sometimes so thickly clustered together that they look like a
planted crop of bright yellow. The seeds are used, as a
matter of fact, along with the seeds of the White Mustard,
another common weed mustard, in the making of condi-
ments, and to express a fine clear oil, which is of a mild
flavor, not sharp. The stems of this mustard grow from
one to seven feet high. The mustards, and especially this
black species, are noxious weeds. The Black Mustard is
coarse and vexatious, and hard to control. Its seeds are very
numerous; over ten thousand of them may come from a
thrifty plant. Other common mustards, more or less like
the Black Mustard, are the Charlock or Wild Mustard,
White Mustard, Ball Mustard, Wild Radish, Indian Mustard, and Sand Rocket. These are all imported weeds, that
thrive readily in our country.

Cinquefoil.   In dry soil of fields, meadows, pastures,
and all sorts of waste places, as well as sometimes in our
garden borders and the borders of paths, one's eye is often
attracted by what looks like little yellow strawberry-like
flowers, growing on a plant with decidedly strawberry-like

FIG. 64—Cinquefoil or Five-finger.

leaves. This is often wrongly called the wild strawberry. It is, however, the Five-finger, or Common Cinquefoil (Fig. 64). The flowers are a delicate pure lemon yellow, and arise thickly on the stems that trail over the ground. Its bright-colored flowers and prettily cut leaves make it a most attractive little plant, and a great favorite in "saucer-gardens" indoors. The cinquefoil is often called Potentilla, a name referring to the supposed powerful (potent) medicinal properties of this plant, and of some of the members of its group.

Dandelion, or Blowballs.   From March throughout the entire summer and well into September the bright golden

FIG. 65—Dandelion.

flowers of the common Dandelion (Fig. 65) are in full bloom. Each flower-head, from one to two inches across, is made of many tiny florets. Soon the Blowballs appear, silvery white globes composed of little downy parachutes which become detached, and float away on the wind, bearing the seeds here and there. The conspicuously toothed, large, green leaves give the plant its common name, Dandelion, which is a corruption of the French name of the plant, *dent-de-lion,* or tooth of a lion. The plant grows as a weed on lawns and open ground generally, was early naturalized from Europe, and has now extended its range over most of the cold and temperate portions of the Northern and Southern Hemispheres. Many people find the leaves good to cook as greens.

Pearly Everlasting or Life Everlasting.   In the late summer these very fragrant pearly-white flowers (Fig. 66) appear in old dry fields and places where there are stretches of sandy soil; sometimes well up on a mountain side. The flat-topped clusters, some six inches across, bear male and female flower heads on separate plants. Each flower head

FIG. 66—Pearly Everlasting.

is composed of many white, scaly petal-like florets, surrounding the central disk of yellow florets. There are three varieties of Pearly Everlasting, which vary according to the smoothness or woolliness of the stems and leaves. The margins of the leaves are rolled inwards. These plants are found from Newfoundland south to North Carolina and west to Alaska, Oregon, and New Mexico.

Selfheal or Heal-All.   Almost universal seems to be the use of Selfheal (Fig. 67) in the making of an ointment for the healing of flesh wounds, and as a medicament for quinsy, for this plant is almost global in its distribution. It

FIG. 67—Selfheal.

is a native originally of the Old World, but now widely distributed. The close flower-spikes, from two to four inches long, bear small violet-colored flowers. Some species bear white, some rose-colored flowers. The plants, two to four inches high, have four-angled, slightly hairy stems. This is one of the commonest weeds of lawns, grasslands, waste places, and roadsides. Selfheal is also known as Prunella.

Ladies' Tresses.   In meadows and low grassy places one often sees a peculiar little plant, consisting of several light green, rather grass-like leaves and a straight stem about as tall or taller, with little white tubular flowers arranged in a sort of twisted way at its top. This twist of the flower-stalk is so unusual that few people pass the blossom by. It is the Ladies' Tresses (Fig. 68), often called in country districts the Wild Hyacinth. This very pretty little orchid (for it belongs to that famous family) may be found growing in great abundance in all sorts of situations, moist and dry. It blooms freely in late August, September, and October. The braided

FIG. 68—Ladies' Tresses.

appearance of the flower spikes gives the plant its name. In earlier times in England its name was, however, Ladies' Traces, in allusion to the resemblance between its twisted flower stalk and the lacings or "traces" which in those days formed so important a part of feminine apparel. Another pretty little plant, much like this one, the Slender Ladies' Tresses, more common in drier situations such as dry hillside pastures, has a few small ovate leaves at the ground level at the base of the flower-stalk. The flowers are like those of the other species, but are smaller and more delicate. They are a creamy white, and very fragrant. Another species is the Grass-leaved Ladies' Tresses, with a leafy stalk, and a heavier stalk of twisted blossoms. These are much more yellow in tone than the flowers of the other two we have mentioned, and spread out more from the stem. All the Ladies' Tresses are easily recognizable in the field.

Shepherd's Purse. Perhaps you have often seen the Shepherd's Purse (Fig. 69), a plant about six inches or a foot and a half high, with tiny white flowers, growing up along roadsides, near dwellings, or on waste ground, and in fields. Perhaps your eye was attracted to the little triangular

FIG. 69—Shepherd's Purse.

seed pods, set upon long stalks. These resemble the purses
worn at the belts of shepherds; hence the name. With the
exception of the chickweed, this is probably the commonest
weed in the world. And no wonder, when you consider that
each one of the little purse-like seed pods contains from ten
to twenty seeds. A large thrifty plant may produce as many
as two thousand of these little reddish-brown seeds. The
seeds have long vitality, and can live several years in the soil
before sprouting. The Shepherd's Purse came from Europe.
Among common names are St. James's Weed, Mothers'
Hearts, Caseweed.

Indian Paint-Brush or Painted-Cup.   The inconspicuous

FIG. 70—Indian Paint-Brush.

greenish-yellow flowers of the Indian Paint-Brush (Fig. 70)
are surrounded by brilliant, showy, three to five-cleft bracts
(modified leaves). Some species possess scarlet, green,
yellow, or white bracts; all these appear to have been dipped
in paint, hence the name of the plant. The slender hairy
stems, from one to two feet tall, arise from a basal rosette of
leaves. The plants partake somewhat of the nature of root
parasites. From June to September one finds the Paint-Brush
growing in peaty meadows, pastures, and damp sandy soils
from New Hampshire south to Florida and west to Manitoba, Oklahoma, and Louisiana.

Thistle.   Throughout all the hot days of summer, and
often well into November, bees and butterflies hover about
the flowers of the Common Thistle or Bull Thistle (Fig.
71), sipping its abundant nectar. The flower heads, which

FIG. 71—Thistle.

vary from light to dark magenta, measure from two to three
inches across, and contain numerous tubular florets. The
plants, from two to five feet tall, bear leaves which are dark
green above, brown-woolly beneath, and armed with very
sharp formidable whitish spines. This very aggressive

biennial weed, an importation from Europe, makes itself quite at home in pastures, clearings, waste places, and along roadsides from Newfoundland south to Florida and west to Minnesota, Nebraska, and Texas.

Yarrow or Milfoil.   The old-fashioned physicians used to gather the flowers and stems of Yarrow (Fig. 72) to use

FIG. 72—Yarrow.

as a general "cure-all" for stopping wounds, for digestive difficulties, and as a general tonic. The minute grayish-white flower-heads with yellow discs form large flat-topped clusters. Rarely the ray florets are pink or deep rose-purple. The grayish-green feathery leaves, from one to ten inches in length, are pungent and aromatic. The plant stems, from one to two feet high, are webby-hairy. Yarrow is a common weed, naturalized from Europe and now well established in fields, meadows, and along roadsides throughout North America, except in the extreme north.

Knotweed or Knot Grass.   There are many different kinds of Knotweeds, but all possess smooth stems thickened at the joints. From July throughout the summer into September the plants are in flower, but the flowers are tiny and inconspicuous. They are greenish yellow in color and hidden in the axils of the leaves, and ordinarily not seen unless searched for. One of the common knotweeds is the species known as the Erect Knotweed (Fig. 73). This plant

FIG. 73—Erect Knotweed.

is seen abundantly in dooryards, waysides, and waste places generally. It is stout, erect, bushily-branched, and has yellowish green leaves. It is a species widely distributed from Ontario southward to Tennessee and westward to Saskatchewan and Ontario.

Mullein. This tall, interesting plant, the Common Mullein (Fig. 74), goes under a great many common

FIG. 74—Common Mullein.

names, such as: Velvet Dock, Feltwort, Jacob's Staff, Blanket-Leaf, Hedge Taper, Candle-Wick Plant, and others. Throughout the summer the tall, stately, stout stalks, from two to seven feet high, bear steeple-like spikes of yellow flowers two-thirds of an inch across. Seedsmen now sell seeds of hybrids whose flowers range from white to yellow, apricot, rose, and violet. Numerous densely woolly, flannel-like leaves grow along the stem and in a rosette at the base of the plant. Country girls redden their cheeks by rubbing them with mullein leaves. The plant is used medicinally for colds, catarrh, and dysentery. It is a native of Europe, but has become naturalized as a familiar weed in old fields, pastures, and waste places from Nova Scotia south to Florida, and west to South Dakota, Kansas, and California.

Goldenrods. The Goldenrods are a vast host of flowering plants, some eighty-five or more being found in our country, and some twenty-five commonly occurring in the

FIG. 75—Late Goldenrod.

northern United States. A common species, the Late Goldenrod (Fig. 75) blooms from midsummer to late fall. Like all goldenrods (except the White Goldenrod, or Silverrod) its blooms are golden yellow. Its straight, smooth, dignified stem is cylindrical in section, and is light green. The stems of the flower-heads are covered with tiny white hairs. This goldenrod grows from three to six or seven feet in height, and is common in copses and dry roadsides everywhere. Other goldenrods will always be encountered by the walker in the fields and woodlands. The White Goldenrod, or Silverrod is a very common species and the only one of the goldenrods bearing white flowers. The general habit of growth is somewhat similar to the other members of its family, and you would have no difficulty in determining it to be a goldenrod. The stem is usually simple, although sometimes branched, upright, and covered with fine gray hairs. The little thickly massed flowers at the top of the stem are tubular and white or cream-colored. The Silverrod grows on dry barren soils, in fields, along roadways, and in waste-lands generally, and is found from Maine southward to Georgia and westward as far as Minnesota and Missouri. A dwarf goldenrod, growing only about six to eight inches high, with stout stems and thick heavy golden flowers, is confined to high mountain tops (the Green Mountains, White Mountains, the Adirondacks, and so on) and is called the Alpine Goldenrod. One of the earliest of the goldenrods to blossom is the Sharp-leaved Goldenrod, or Summer Goldenrod. This bears very light golden-yellow flowers, arranged in soft plume-like clusters. The stem is angled, smooth, and varies from green to ruddy brown. The deep green leaves are indistinctly feather-veined, large, thin, and coarsely toothed. This goldenrod reaches a height of two to four feet. Another early goldenrod, often found growing in company with the foregoing species, is the Early Goldenrod (or Summer Goldenrod). This may be identified by its smooth, yellow-olive-green leaves, which are slightly three-ribbed; the upper leaves are toothless, the lower ones broadly lance-shaped.

Asters.   Like the goldenrods, the asters are a very numerous tribe. Like the goldenrods, too, they are found in abundance along the byways and roadsides in autumn. They are clustered, bushy-looking, daisy-like plants, their little blossoms being white, lavender, or bluish. The loveliest of all the wild asters, the New England Aster (Fig. 76), is a

FIG. 76—New England Aster.

common species, rising up to a height of two to six feet, and bearing large purple or magenta-pink very showy flowers. This is so beautiful a species that it is frequently cultivated in gardens. The New York Aster, or Willow-leaved Blue Aster, is somewhat similar, with large pale violet or lilac flowers. This is the commonest late-flowering aster of the Atlantic coastal region, commoner than the New England Aster, and very variable in its color. It grows from a foot or so to about three feet in height. One of the famous asters of our country is the Heath Aster or Michaelmas Daisy (blooming at the time of Michaelmas, and forming dense shows of massed bloom from September to November). This is a tiny white aster, its white flowers bearing little yellow centers, and looking like miniature daisies. This aster has spread widely from its natural limits, through its cultivation by bee-keepers, for its yield of nectar is very large, and hence the plant is a special favorite of the honey-bee. It grows from one to three feet or more in height, and is found along roadsides, paths, and dry fields generally, from Maine southward to southern New England, New Jersey, and thence westward to Kentucky and Wisconsin. Another similar aster possesses a hairy instead of a smooth stem; this is the Many-flowered Aster. Its blossoms are more apt to be tinted with lilac than those of the white-flowered Heath Aster.

Common Milkweed or Silkweed. This species is the commonest of all the many milkweeds (Fig. 77), and its

FIG. 77—Common Milkweed.

pendulous clusters of pale lilac or dull purple flowers are heavily fragrant. The stems and leaves are finely downy. Young shoots and tender young pods of this plant are delicious when cooked as one would cook asparagus. This

milkweed is common everywhere but especially along country roadsides and in old dry fields, from New Brunswick
south to Georgia and west to Saskatchewan and Tennessee.
There are several species of milkweeds, all possessing a
heavy milky juice. Their flowers vary in color from greenish
white and cream-white to magenta-pink and dull crimson.
But the most brilliant of the family is the very showy orange-
yellow flowered Butterfly-weed or Pleurisy-root, found
growing in dry fields, and also as a cultivated plant in gardens.

St. John's-Wort.   Throughout the summer the Common
St. John's-Wort (Fig. 78) puts forth its numerous flat-

Fig. 78—Common St. John's-Wort.

topped clusters of deep orange-yellow shiny flowers. These
are sometimes gathered to make a healing "red oil". The
flowers, about two-thirds to one inch across, are often
black-dotted on the margins of the petals. The dull green
leaves bear numerous transparent dots which are readily
seen when the leaves are held up against the light. The
plants may attain a height of from two to three feet, and
are much branched. The stems are stiff, tough, and two-
edged. This Common St. John's-Wort is a weed which has

come to our country from Asia by way of Europe, and has made itself very commonly at home in dry pastures, neglected fields, and along our roadsides everywhere.

Fireweed or Great Willow-Herb.   This is one of several plants which always follow fires, appearing in burned-over areas and clearings. In the very heart of London, after the severe bombings of World War II, Fireweed (Fig. 79) suddenly appeared where it had not grown before for many

FIG. 79—Fireweed.

decades. The flowers are from two-thirds to one and a quarter inches across; they are usually light magenta, but sometimes pink or white. The plants are perennial, from two to eight feet in height, and grow massed together in thick showy patches. The long willow-like leaves have prominent white mid-veins. The stems and the seed-pods are usually purplish. Fireweed grows from Greenland and Newfoundland south to the mountains of North Carolina, and west to Alaska, California, and Arizona.

Bouncing Bet or Soapwort.   Bouncing Bet (Fig. 80) is a rank-growing plant which puts forth—during the period from June to September—flat-topped clusters of spicy delicate magenta-pink and white flowers. Some of these are single, some double, and measure about an inch across. The

FIG. 80—Bouncing Bet.

leaves and stems are very smooth; the latter, which grow up from one to two feet high, are stout and thick-jointed. The juice of the plant is very mucilaginous producing a copious lather when mingled with water; hence one of the plant's common names is Soapwort. In the early days of our country this was widely used in the washing of fine fabrics. The Bouncing-Bet is not a native American, but was early introduced into this country from the Old World, and soon spread rapidly. It is now found growing throughout all of eastern North America, and has become an extremely common wild flower along roadsides, railroad embankments, in waste places, around old cellar holes; and it is still raised in old-fashioned gardens.

WILD FLOWERS OF WOODLANDS AND MOIST EDGES OF WOODS

Wild Violets.   The violets are well-known, but their different kinds are not so well-known. Our commonest one,

perhaps, is the one which the walker sees along roadsides
and in fields and meadows everywhere. When one says "a
violet," one usually means the Common Violet (or Butter-
fly Violet, which is the translation of its Latin name, *Viola
papilionacea*). The leaves of this violet are heart-shaped,
either drawn out, or else rather broad and fat. Much like
this violet is another common one, the Arrow-leaved Violet
(Fig. 81). The chief difference is that in the Common
Violet the leaves are broad, and in the Arrow-leaved Violet
the leaves are like arrowheads. These leaves, also, when

FIG. 81—Arrow-leaved Violet.

seen in masses, show a slight silvery grayish bloom. The
Common Violet flowers vary in color from light purple to
pale violet, or deep violet. Very rarely they may be white
or whitish with purplish or violet veins. The plants rise up
to a height of two to eight inches. The Arrow-leaved Violet
flowers are a light to a deep violet (almost never purple),
and the whole plant is smaller and more delicate than the
other. Other violets are the tiny Sweet White Violet, the
Downy Yellow Violet, the Round-leaved Violet, and the
Bird-foot Violet, with its leaves delicately cut like birds'
feet.

Wood Lily.   The lovely orange-scarlet lily that one sees in damp situations, or in wet woodlands, and which even the most careless observer of nature sees with a thrill of pleasure, is the Wood Lily (Fig. 82), often also called the

FIG. 82—Wood Lily.

Orange-Red Wood Lily. This is our most brilliantly colored wild lily, with bright green very leafy stems, and with the flower cup opening upward, not drooping. The six petals narrow to a slender stem-like base. The usual color is a brilliant orange-scarlet, but it varies from this hue through scarlet-orange to a paler shade of the same, and is spotted with purplish-brown on the inner part of the blossom-cup. The flowers are borne singly or in twos or threes, at the summit of the plant stem.

Hepatica.   The Hepatica (Fig. 83) is the earliest flower of spring, appearing before its new leaves (though often the old ones may be found lying prostrate and dead). Its delicate flowers are white, bluish, violet, or pinkish, but their form identifies them. The leaves of the plant look somewhat like lobes of the human liver, hence the names Hepatica and Liverleaf. This lovely little blossom will usually be found

FIG. 83—Hepatica.

half hidden in the leaves that cover the forest floor, or tucked away among loose rocks.

Bloodroot.   In the very early spring, along the borders of woodlands, and along woodland roadsides and paths and trails, one sees the pure white blossoms of the Bloodroot (Fig. 84) shining out like large silver stars, looking all

FIG. 84—Bloodroot.

the more striking because of the bare brown earth and dark slate-gray leafless twigs of the shrubs and bushes nearby. The stem of the flower reaches up, often, through the folded leaf. There are sometimes eight, or rarely twelve, pure white petals, and a bunch of pretty, golden-orange anthers. Break off the plant near the base, and from the end exudes a bright orange-red juice—hence the name Bloodroot. The root bleeds with a much redder sap. This is one of our earliest flowers of spring. The blossom attracts many kinds of insects which gather pollen, but which find no nectar in the flower. Its chief insect visitors—prominent callers in the bleak days of early spring—are bumblebees, honeybees, some smaller bees (of the genus Halictus), and the bee-flies, Bombylius.

Spring Beauty.   In damp woodlands in the early spring the ground is often almost carpeted with a low-growing, rather grass-like plant with long, delicate, dark-green leaves and pretty little pinkish or white flowers in masses. This is the Spring Beauty, or Claytonia (Fig. 85). The color of the

Fig. 85—Spring Beauty or Claytonia.

flower varies from pure white to delicate pink. The petals are often veined with darker pink, or crimson. Another name for it is Mayflower. The Spring Beauty is widely distributed from Maine south to Georgia and west as far as Texas.

Dutchman's Breeches.   One of the queerest of all our woodland blossoms, as well as one of the prettiest and most delicate, is the Dutchman's Breeches (Dicentra) (Fig. 86).

FIG. 86—Dutchman's Breeches.

It may be known at once, even before it flowers, by its unusual, feathery, compound leaf which is long-stemmed,
growing directly from the root. It is thin and grayish, almost
a sage-green, and somewhat bluish-green and paler on the
under side. The flowers nod on their stalks, and are white,
with their spurs tinted with yellow. In form they look like
what the name implies. The Climbing Fumitory, or Mountain Fringe, is somewhat similar in its blossoms, but these
are white, tinted with magenta-pink, never yellow. Moreover, the plant is in the form of a delicate vine, climbing
and trailing over thickets and low shrubbery.

Adder's Tongue. Very common in moist woodlands,
particularly in little brook valleys and watered glades, is the
early spring flower, Adder's Tongue (Fig. 87). The flower
appears after the leaves, and is a dull golden-yellow inside,
and a brownish-purple outside, this shade varying somewhat. The two leaves of the plant are usually mottled
prettily with shades of brownish-purple; hence one of its
common names—Trout Lily. This is a good name, for the
plant belongs to the Lily Family, and is not a violet, as another of its common names, Dog-tooth Violet, might lead

FIG. 87—Adder's Tongue.

one to believe. Much visited in early spring by the queen bumblebee, Bombus.

Trillium or Wake Robin. In rich woodlands everywhere, one finds also the very common three-petalled Wake Robin or Trillium (Fig. 88). You will often find it blossom-

FIG. 88—Trillium or Wake Robin.

ing from early April to mid-June. Before you find it, you may notice, in its neighborhood, its ill odor; hence another common name—Stinking Benjamin. The flower is sometimes a dull pink, but usually it is some shade of maroon. Rarely is it white. The plant grows from six to sixteen inches high.

Anemone. Very common everywhere in scattered woodlands is the very delicate Rue Anemone (Fig. 89).

FIG. 89—Rue Anemone.

The word Anemone means "windflower." The lovely blossom, usually white, but sometimes tinged with magenta or pink, has orange-yellow stamens. Grows to four or eight inches.

Columbine. The Columbine (Fig. 90) is the delicate, tall scarlet and yellow flower seen on wooded hillsides and

FIG. 90—Columbine.

the borders of wooded glens. It grows to a height of one to two feet. The petals are in the form of five tubes, which end in spurs where the nectar collects. The nectar is reached only by long-tongued insects. Some insects bite through the little bulb at the tip of the spur, and thus secure the nectar without fertilizing the flower.

Trailing Arbutus or Mayflower.   One of the first flowers of springtime is the Trailing Arbutus (Fig. 91), the May-flower of the Pilgrims. The delicate fragrant pink and white flowers appear among last year's dull bronzy-green rust-spotted leaves, which are rough and bristly. New green leaves appear after the flowers. The prostrate stems creep along the ground to a length of from six to fifteen inches.

Fig. 91—Trailing Arbutus.

Arbutus is rare and is fast disappearing; hence it should be gathered only when abundant, and even then should be cut (not pulled up) sparingly. Arbutus is found in woodlands and along their borders, from Labrador south to Florida, and westward to Saskatchewan, Wisconsin, and Tennessee. There are only two species of Arbutus in the world: our species, and one found in Japan. Once in a while a smoothed-leaved or double-flowered variety is found.

Jack-in-the-Pulpit.   The curious structure of the flower parts of the Jack-in-the-Pulpit (Fig. 92) attracts the eye in woodlands and damp situations everywhere. The leaves are

FIG. 92—Jack-in-the-Pulpit.

large and tall and very showy, and the flower is almost as tall and quite distinctive. The little flowers, grouped at the bottom of a club-like structure (called the spadix) are generally staminate and pistillate on separate plants—that is, the stamens are undeveloped on one plant, and the pistils are undeveloped on another plant. The unusual and beautiful hood, or "pulpit cover," that arches over and protects the spadix (the "Jack" in his pulpit) is green, striped with purplish-brown, although these colors may vary a good deal. But no one can mistake this little woodland preacher in his pulpit, no matter what the colors! The fruit is a lovely cluster of brilliant coral-red berries. Try tasting a little sliver of the roundish, potato-like bulb, but do so cautiously, for it is exceedingly peppery and fiery! When dried, it may be ground up into a flour which makes a nutritious and very palatable thick soup or sort of bread. The Indians used it thus as food; hence one of the plant's names, Indian Potato, or Indian Turnip.

Wild Geranium or Spotted Cranesbill.   From April onward through the month of June, the Wild Geranium (Fig. 93) puts forth terminal clusters of fragrant magenta-pink

FIG. 93—Wild Geranium.

(rarely white) flowers each from one to one and a half inches across. These are the true Geraniums. The house-plants which are commonly called "Geraniums" are really Pelargoniums. The plants of the Wild Geranium attain a height of from one to two feet. The leaves, from three to six inches across, are spotted with brown and white. Both the leaf-stems and the sepals are hairy. These very decorative plants may be found in woodlands, thickets, and along roadsides from Maine south to Georgia and west to Manitoba, Kansas, and Texas.

Solomon's Seal.   In thickets, along roadsides, in woodland glades and clearings in the forest, and on the sides of

FIG. 94—Solomon's Seal.

mountain trails, one finds very often the characteristic wavy-stemmed, alternate-leaved Solomon's Seal (Fig. 94). Its deeply veined leaves are very decorative, as are also its un-usual little bell-like, twin flowers, hanging two by two from near the bases of the leaves. They are pale green, or whitish, and later give place to blue-black berries.

False Solomon's Seal.   A little flower of midspring is the Canada Mayflower, often called the False Solomon's Seal, although it is of an entirely different family than the true Solomon's Seal, and Wild Lily of the Valley (Fig. 95). This

FIG. 95—False Solomon's Seal.

tiny woodland plant is a great favorite with walkers in the woods. It is easily gathered, and lasts a long time in a minia-ture bouquet. Moreover, it is very common, often carpeting the ground with its delicate, foamy white flowers. It some-what resembles the little Three-leaved Canada Mayflower, or Three-leaved False Solomon's Seal, but has two leaves on its little erect stem instead of three. Both these little plants are very common in woodlands and hill- and moun-tainsides, in the woods, from Maine southward as far as Maryland, and westward.

Lady's Slipper.   The orchids have attracted lovers of the out-of-doors for centuries! Nearly every walker in the woods knows the commonest one, the Lady's Slipper, or Moccasin Flower (Fig. 96). Its two large lily-like leaves spring

FIG. 96—Lady's Slipper or Moccasin Flower.

directly from the root, without a stem, a fact that accounts for another of its common names, Stemless Lady's Slipper. The pouch of the flower is crimson-pink, sometimes darker, sometimes almost white. The flower may be seven to fourteen inches high.

Wood Sorrel.   One of the daintiest of all our woodland blossoms is the pretty white, pink-veined Wood Sorrel, or Wood Oxalis (Fig. 97). This grows in cool damp situations in woodlands, particularly in mountain woodlands. The

FIG. 97—Wood Sorrel or Wood Oxalis.

leaves are light green and fold together after nightfall. The
fragile little flowers are white, delicately veined with pink.
The whole plant is only three or four inches tall.

Clintonia. The slender, very graceful, large-leaved
Clintonia (Fig. 98) is often seen by the climber on mountain trails in the woods. The flowers rise up to a height of
eight to sixteen inches or more, and the very showy glossy

FIG. 98—Clintonia.

green leaves are nearly that height. The berries which follow
the blossoms are a vivid deep blue—said to be the purest
blue in the plant world.

Early Saxifrage.   In rocky places, sometimes on cliffs,
one sees little rosettes of leaves, from the center of which
spring long flower-stalks, from three to eight inches or so
in height. The tiny whitish or greenish-white flowers are
among the earliest of our spring blossoms. This little plant
is the Early (or Rock) Saxifrage (Fig. 99). The name
comes from the Latin, *saxifragus,* meaning "breaker of
rocks," for the roots of the plants penetrate into every crev-
ice on the rock where they may be trying to secure a pre-
carious foot-hold. The flowers are followed by attractive
madder-purple seed capsules.

FIG. 99—Early Saxifrage.

Spring Cress. Alongside of springs on the edges of woodlands, or in little wet woodland glades, grows the pretty, delicate Spring Cress (Fig. 100). Its flowers are

FIG. 100—Spring Cress.

white, and about half an inch in length. Another common variety of this early cress is the Purple Cress, with pale magenta-purple flowers and a slightly woolly stem. This blooms a bit earlier.

False Spikenard. The False Spikenard (Fig. 101) is a well-known flower of May. It grows from one to three feet tall and is common in moist woodlands and beside woodland roadways. The pretty leaves attract attention before and after the white foamy flower-head has appeared. After

FIG. 101—False Spikenard.

the flower comes a cluster of bright red soft berries. This plant resembles the famous Solomon's Seal in its general growth habit. In the latter plant the flowers are borne in the angles (axils) of the leaves.

Toothwort. Often overlooked is the Toothwort, or Crinkleroot (Fig. 102), for it is such a common plant. Its

FIG. 102—Toothwort.

flowers are not especially attractive or distinctive, being white and relatively inconspicuous (only about two-thirds of an inch wide when fully opened). It is a rather tall plant, however, from eight or ten inches to about a foot or more high. Its root is interesting, being crinkled or toothed, and is edible, possessing an agreeable, pungent, mildly peppery flavor, somewhat like that of a mild watercress. A similar kind of toothwort, the Cut-leaved Toothwort, is often chanced upon by the woodland stroller. The leaves of this species are deeply cut into narrow lobes, and the flowers, while sometimes white, are more often delicately tinged with magenta-pink. The root of this plant is also peppery and edible.

Mandrake. A lovely plant which is a common sight in moist woodland glades has large leaves which look like umbrellas. They may sometimes measure nearly a foot in

FIG. 103—Mandrake.

diameter. This is the Mandrake, or May Apple (Fig. 103), sometimes also called the Umbrella Leaf, or—in allusion to its lemon-like, edible fruit, the Wild Lemon. The flower droops from between two leaves, is white, and rather ill-scented. The fruit is edible, but to some slightly poisonous; the rest of the plant is decidedly poisonous; it is used, however, in certain medicines.

Rattlesnake Plantain. The leaves of the Rattlesnake Plantain (Fig. 104) never fail to arrest the attention of the walker in the woodlands. They are a dark bluish olive-

FIG. 104—Rattlesnake Plantain.

green, with white veins, the middle vein being the largest. The plant is gathered for ferneries, for its leaf-rosette is the prettiest part of the plant. The flower stalk rises up from six to twelve inches high, and is woolly. At its summit are the small flowers, which are white, creamy white, or greenish, rarely flesh-color. There are several of the rattlesnake plantains but all may be recognized by the reticulated patterns on their leaves. The rattlesnake plantains belong to the Orchid Family.

Pipsissewa or Prince's Pine.   This mid-summer flower is waxy, very fragrant, and a white or pale pink color with

FIG. 105—Pipsissewa.

showy magenta stamens. Pipsissewas (Fig. 105) grow up
to a height of from six to twelve inches, and bear two whorls
of thick dark shining evergreen leaves. They grow in rather
dry woods, mostly under some species of evergreen tree—
usually pine, hemlock, or spruce—where their shining
leaves offer a pretty contrast to the bed of brown or dull
gray dry needles from which they spring. Pipsissewa, to give
the plant its pleasing Indian name, is widely distributed
from the Gaspé Peninsula and Quebec south to Georgia and
west to Ontario, Michigan, and Illinois. Similar to the Pipsissewa is the Spotted Wintergreen with showy white-veined
evergreen leaves.

Indian-Pipe. In mid-summer appear these nodding,
solitary, waxy-white, ghostly sort of flowers, Indian-Pipes
(Fig. 106), shining out conspicuously in the dark rich

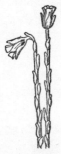

FIG. 106—Indian-Pipe.

woodlands. Rarely the plant is fleshy-pink or even reddish,
especially in late summer. The plants blacken when gathered. The ripened seed-pod is held erect. Indian-Pipes (also
called Corpse-Plant) grow up from four to ten inches high
and have peculiar waxy stems and white scaly bracts instead

of leaves. The ball of fibrous rootlets is parasitic on growing plants or on decomposing vegetable matter in the soil. Indian-Pipes are found in North America as well as in Mexico, Japan, and the Himalaya Mountains.

Partridge-berry, Twinberry, or Two-Eyed-Berry.   The deliciously fragrant faint-perfumed flowers of this creeping plant grow in pairs close together with their ovaries united, thus producing a berry-like bright-red fruit with two little "eyes" at one end. The flowers, which appear from April

FIG. 107—Partridge-berry.

through July, are creamy white, densely hairy within, and crimson-pink and smooth without. The Partridge-berry (Fig. 107) is a creeping plant, which roots at the nodes, and produces pretty, ovate dark-green, evergreen leaves with white veins. The Patridge-berry grows in moist woodlands from Nova Scotia south to Florida and west to Ontario, Minnesota, and Texas. Another closely allied species is found in Japan.

Bunchberry or Dwarf Cornel.   This small plant is nevertheless a true dogwood, and closely related to the trees of that name. The flowers of the Bunchberry (Fig. 108) appear from May to July; they are very numerous, tiny green-

FIG. 108—Bunchberry.

ish or creamy in color, clustered together and surrounded by four large showy greenish-white modified leaves which are called bracts. These little flowers give rise later in August and October to compact clusters of brilliant scarlet berry-like fruits. The flowering stems are about three to nine inches high. Bunchberry grows from creeping underground stems in cool damp woods from Greenland and Labrador south to West Virginia; west to Alaska, California and New Mexico.

Wintergreen, Checkerberry, or Teaberry. From this plant is obtained the true oil of wintergreen used in flavoring candies, medicines, rubbing oils. The oil of birch is also

FIG. 109—Wintergreen.

used for these purposes, since it is almost identical in flavor. Wintergreen (Fig. 109) is aromatic throughout the entire plant: leaves, flowers, and fruits. From June to August appear white waxy flowers, each about a quarter of an inch long, which later produce deep cherry-red berries, full of flavor and beloved of children and grown-ups alike. In the spring the tender, bronzy-green new leaves, called pips, make excellent aromatic browzing. Later in the season the leaves become shining, leathery, dark evergreen. In winter they often turn to a ruddy hue. Creeping underground stems send up shoots, thus producing large patches of these evergreen plants. Wintergreen is a plant of sterile dry sandy woods and clearings, and is found abundantly from Newfoundland south to Georgia and Alabama, and west to Manitoba and Indiana.

WILD FLOWERS AND PLANTS OF THE WEST AND SOUTH

Opuntias. The Opuntias, or Prickly Pear Cactuses (Fig. 110) run over the ground, sometimes singly, some-

FIG. 110—Opuntia or Prickly Pear Cactus.

times in mats, with their much-flattened, green, thick joints often covered with large yellow flowers. These measure some three or four inches across. The petals may often be variously tinted, on the outside, with shades of deeper yellow, salmon, rose, or even pale brown. There are some fifty or more kinds of the Prickly Pears, many of them not definitely classified. They range widely in the West, and are found straggling as far as the southern New England States.

Evening Snow.   On open slopes and hills of the west one sees in the early spring the exceedingly pretty little Evening Snow, or Linanthus (Fig. 111). The flowers are readily

FIG. 111—Evening Snow.

found, for they are an inch or even more across, in form rather salver-shaped, and beautifully shiny-white in texture. On the outside the petals are a delicate brownish-pink, showing where they overlapped while in the bud. They have a strong and, to most nostrils, a rather unpleasant odor, but their effect in masses is very beautiful, particularly if they happen to be growing in a rather desert place. They sway to and fro in the wind on their slender but tough stems, showing first their glistening inside, and then their tinted outside. They open only towards evening, and remain open all night, and thus keep on opening and closing for several days or a week, growing larger all the time. The stems are brown, and the whole plant grows to a height of three inches to a little over a foot.

Rock Rose. Another very attractive little bushy sort of plant, of the far west, is the Rock Rose (Fig. 112), with its five-petalled yellow flower—that is, the petals are yellow, but the sepals beneath are pinkish or reddish. The central pistil is green, or brownish-green. There are many slender stems, and a multitude of narrow, yellowish-green leaves on the entire plant. The plants form clumps or more open bushes, from one to two feet high, feathery in appearance,

FIG. 112—Rock Rose.

and resembling very often clumps of large grass sprinkled with flowers. The Helianthemum group, to which this Rock Rose belongs, is often also called the Sun Rose group, and is interesting commercially since many of these herbs or diffusedly growing low shrub-like plants are well adapted to border plantings, or rock gardens, as ground-cover. Some have yellow flowers (as our present species), some white, some rose, some various shades of lavender and purple. The Rock Rose, as well as others of its group, should be looked for in open sunny situations, on rather dry limestone soils. One member of the group, the Variable Sun Rose, is very hardy, and is found in rock gardens in the north in many lovely variations. (This is *Helianthemum variabile,* or *Heli-*

anthemum nummularium). Of this there are some eight or nine varieties.

Harebell. In the higher altitudes of the western hills and mountains, one comes across one of the prettiest and most delicate, as well as one of the most common of all the widely ranging blue flowers, the delicate Harebell, or Campanula (Fig. 113). Nearly everyone has seen these large

FIG. 113—Harebell.

rich blue blossoms. They flower at high altitudes in great profusion, and in late summer form conspicuous blue areas on the uplands. Although rather large, the flowers are fragile, and one hardly expects them to appear at such heights, or to persist where such severe cold and burning-hot sun alternately subject them to very rigorous conditions. Yet they survive, and one finds them adapting themselves to all the varying conditions found from the lower foothills to the tops, almost, of the highest peaks. Their favorite haunts are moist places. They are especially at home in rifts in canyon walls, and on exposed ledges.

Pasque Flower. In the foothills of our midwestern

mountains, as well as widely distributed from Illinois westward, we find one of the best-loved of all the early spring flowers—the lovely purple or whitish Pasque Flower (Fig. 114). These are so common that their name is on everyone's lips in the spring. When the flower buds first arise in late February or early March they resemble little gray kittens, being covered with a soft furry gray coat. The plant grows up as a single flower directly from an underground stem, the leaves coming after the flower has opened. The

FIG. 114—Pasque Flower.

flower is peculiar in that it possesses only sepals and no petals, these forming the showy part of the blossom. Below the colored sepals is a circle of fine hairy narrow bracts. The Pasque Flower is also known as the Anemone, in the west. It grows chiefly in coarse soil, and hence is not a flower of the open plains, but occurs in hilly regions, or in the foothills of the mountains, and sometimes climbs the mountains even as high as the timber-line.

White-flowered Evening Primrose. On the plains of Colorado and neighboring states in May, a very striking floral display is afforded by the low-growing, White-flowered Evening Primrose (Fig. 115). These can best be recognized by the fact that no other low-growing plant of the region

FIG. 115—White-flowered Evening Primrose.

produces such large white blossoms, for the petals may be as large as tablespoons, and the whole blossom as large as a small hand. These lovely blooms are not scattered singly, or even in small companies, but are usually massed together by the thousands. The leaves are clustered thickly about the base of the plant. They remind one somewhat of the leaves of a dandelion. The sepals are curved and drooping underneath the white petals, and are of a pretty pale green or yellowish-green color.

Loco Weeds.   The Loco Weeds (Fig. 116) are many in number. They are most abundant in Asia, but many are

FIG. 116—Loco Weed.

found in our West also. They may be recognized by the pea-like flowers (they are, in fact, members of the Pea Family,

Leguminoseae), which are borne on separate, rather long flowerstalks. After the flowers come numerous pods. These are even more striking than the flowers, for they are more or less two-celled, often inflated so that the wind can distribute their small seeds. Hence the plants are often known as rattle weeds. Another name is Milk Vetch. Many kinds are poisonous to horses and cattle. Grazing animals often eat the plant because of its sweet taste. It produces a nervous disorder (hence the name Loco Weed, from the Latin *loco*, meaning "crazy"), and often death.

Senecios. In the west, in late summer and autumn, are to be seen many different kinds of Senecios, or Butterweeds. They all belong to the great Compositae Family, together with the dandelion, daisy, aster, and others. The Yellow Butterweed (Fig. 117) is a plant bearing many of these bright yellow heads. As the heads fade and the fruits ma-

Fig. 117—Senecio or Yellow Butterweed.

ture, the heads become covered with white hairs, hence the name, Senecio, from the Latin, *senex*, meaning "old man." They range from the foothills up the mountains to the timber-line. There are sixty-six kinds of butterweeds in Colorado.

Trumpets.   In the bogs of the south, and west to Louisiana, those who are familiar with the northern Pitcher Plant will be at once attracted to another kind of pitcher plant, the Trumpets (Fig. 118). Trumpets are really elongate-

FIG. 118—Trumpets or Yellow Pitcher Plant.

leaved pitcher plants. The trumpet-shaped leaves stand nearly erect, and the flowers are a light brownish-yellow, or dull yellow, their petals long and drooping. The leaves are a bright green only when growing in bright sunlit situations. Like the leaves of our northern Pitcher Plant, the leaves of the Trumpets entrap inquisitive insects. The outer surface of the trumpet is smooth, but the inner surface is covered with fine bristly hairs, which, pointing downward, prevent insects from crawling out. Within the trumpets they die and disintegrate; their bodies may then be utilized as sources of food.

Water Hyacinth.   In our Florida lagoons and streams one sees the surface of the water sometimes covered with vegetation whose leaves float the plants about by reason of large inflated bladders which are the petioles of the leaves themselves. This is the Water Hyacinth (Fig. 119). The

FIG. 119—Water Hyacinth.

roots of the plant are large and delicately feathery. The flowers are large and showy, and vary in color from light blue to violet, with a blue patch on the upper lobe bearing a yellow spot. A variety of this hyacinth, the Large Water Hyacinth, bears rose, or rose-lilac flowers. This very pretty plant, with its interesting and unusual inflated bladders and its showy blossoms, is a terrible pest in the Florida waterways, clogging them up with great rapidity. It is a native of tropical America, and was early introduced into Florida. Water Hyacinths are often grown as ornamentals in ponds and tanks.

Spanish Moss.   All along our southern seaboard, from Florida to Texas and into tropical America, one sees the trees draped and festooned with long swinging, graceful, soft, grayish-green festoons and trailing tails of the pretty Spanish Moss or Florida Moss (Fig. 120). This plant is not

FIG. 120—Spanish Moss, with flower shown to the left.

a moss at all, however, but is a member of the higher order
of seed plants; in fact, it is a member of the Pineapple Family (Bromeliaceae), and is one of the most numerous of all
the American epiphytic plants—that is, plants which grow
on another plant for elevated support, but draw no part of
their nourishment from the supporting plant, which is usually a tree. The long slender stems and leaves of the Florida
Moss are thickly powdered all over with a silvery scurf. The
festoons of leaves sag in pretty intertwined masses from
three feet to sometimes nearly twenty feet in length. They
are especially common on the Live Oaks, Sycamores, and
Cypresses, although they also occur on other trees. The
leaves are so long and narrow that they are hardly distin-
guishable from the slender stems, and the flowers, also long
and linear, are usually overlooked by the casual observer.
Look among the tangled masses of threadlike stems and
leaves and you will often find the yellowish-brown flowers.
The sepals and petals are long and leaf-like. The Florida or
Spanish Moss, or Silver Moss, is known to botanists sometimes as Tillandsia, and sometimes as Dendropogon. In our
southern states it is sometimes cultivated in gardens for its
picturesqueness, and grown commercially for packing material and for upholstery-stuffing bulk.

Pyxie Moss. From New Jersey southward to North
Carolina, in a narrow zone, there is to be found one of the
most remarkable plants on the North American continent,
and one that many persons must see as they frequent the
curious pine barren tracts of the country on our southern
and southeastern coast. This is a little moss-like plant, running over the ground and often forming mats of small green
or reddish-brown leaves. The mats may be as large as a
saucer, or may cover a foot or more in area; the smaller

mats are the more common. This plant's name is Pyxie, or
Pyxie Moss (Fig. 121). Its pretty pale pinkish or white

FIG. 121—Pyxie Moss.

flowers are thickly sown over the plant like little stars. It is
a most striking plant, as well as a beautiful one. Sometimes
it grows on the embankments of sandy roads.

Guide to American Trees

Those who love the country should know the trees with which they are surrounded. No other single feature of the landscape (except perhaps the hills and mountains) adds so much to the beauty and interest of country life. Some trees are large, some small, some are evergreen, some are green only during the months of summer; but each tree has its own characteristics of leaf, mode of branching, contour or shape, and height, which makes it easy for a beginner to learn the names of the common trees, at least. To know the names of a score or so of common trees is like knowing as many human friends, and the trees, with their quiet, dignified beauty, make the countryside a more likable, friendly place. Forests mean a great deal to our country, and should mean a great deal to each one of us. Forests preserve the land surface from destructive wear and erosion; they conserve our water supply; they furnish us with timber, paper, plastics, and many other articles of commerce, as well as with fruits and other kinds of food. But better than all these things they furnish us with beauty and our minds with an abiding interest.

EVERGREENS

White Pine. One of our very finest northern evergreens, and one of the finest of all our trees, both for beauty and for timber is the White Pine (Fig. 122). It sometimes reaches a height of 100 to 150 feet or more. The branches are rather plume-like, and sweep upward in graceful curves. They are arranged in regular whorls around the trunk. The trunks of most trees are straight, but in others they are picturesquely bent and rugged. The leaves, or needles, are arranged in

FIG. 122—White Pine.

clusters of fives and are a soft bluish-green (not a yellow-green, as in the Pitch Pine). They are slender, flexible, graceful, and angled, and are from three to five inches in length. This magnificent tree ranges from Canada southward along the Alleghany Mountains into Georgia and westward into Iowa. The form of the cones is very distinctive, and, when found lying on the ground under a tree, help greatly in identifying the tree.

Pitch Pine.   Another pine tree is the small evergreen, or conifer, about thirty to forty feet in height, called the Pitch Pine (Fig. 123). The branches are rough and coarse, and often bent and twisted in a picturesque fashion. Sometimes they bear many old blackish cones. The trunk is also coarse and rough, and often bears little tufts of green needles scattered over it; this is especially true of the older trees. On

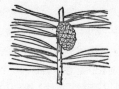

FIG. 123—Pitch Pine.

these older trees, too, the bark is usually cracked up into deep, flat, ragged ridges, thickly covered with dark reddish-brown scales and smaller flakes. The leaves or needles are much stiffer than those of the White Pine, and of a cheerful yellow-green color, rather than a bluish-green. They are set in little stiff clusters of three, and spread out usually more or less at right angles to the twigs from which they arise. They are from two and a half to about four and a half inches long usually. The cones are shorter and fatter than those of the White Pine; rather egg-shaped, sometimes almost round, and when young are of a light brown color. The cone-scales themselves bear, at their tips, sharp curved, short spines. Pitch Pines ordinarily grow on rather poor, often sandy, soil, and range from eastern Canada westward to Ontario, and thence southward.

Larch.   Also called the Tamarack or Hackmatack, the

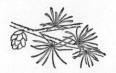

FIG. 124—Larch or Tamarack.

Larch (Fig. 124) is a tall, graceful slender, often steeple-like tree, with rather small, often drooping, branches. In old trees, and where they are growing in the midst of other trees, these branches often spread out in a very irregular and twisty way, on all sides, or one side of the tree. The twigs are a lovely orange-brown (sometimes almost reddish or dark flesh-color) but grow darker with age. The bark is smooth, cracking up later into roundish, thin, reddish-brown scales. The little leaves or needles are very soft and delicate and occur in rather dense clusters at the ends of the short twigs. They are about three-quarters of an inch to an inch and a quarter in length, and are a pretty bright green color, without any bluish tinge. This tree, unlike the other evergreens or conifers, sheds its needles in the fall, like the so-called broad-leaved or deciduous trees. In the spring the fine, delicate, light yellow-green needles come out simultaneously with the young light reddish cones—a very pretty sight indeed. The cones are oval, less than an inch in length, with thin, roundish, papery scales. The Larch is to be looked for in swamps and low damp situations generally, and ranges from Canada southward into Maryland, Indiana, Illinois, and Minnesota.

Spruce.   One of our common northern trees is the Red Spruce (Fig. 125), which extends along the higher moun-

FIG. 125—Red Spruce.

tains southward. It is a valuable timber tree on account of its tall straight trunk. Many masts of sailing vessels have been made of the trunks of these spruces, as well as flagpoles, and the like. The tree is also much prized as an ornamental tree. The twigs are rather hairy and are a yellowish-green, changing to a reddish-brown. As they grow older they acquire a dark brown hue. In all stages they are smooth. The branches extend almost straight out from the trunk, but in some very old trees they droop somewhat. The bark of middle-aged and old trees is cracked into irregular dark brown, or reddish-brown, or dark grayish scales. The needles often extend out on all sides of the twigs; they are deep green in color, rather blunt-pointed, and shine as though covered with a thin varnish. They range from less than half an inch to about an inch in length. The cones may be conveniently used to identify this tree. They are ovoid, light brown (the older ones are much darker), and usually measure about two inches long. The outer edges of the scales are irregular and possess little shallow lobes, but are not sharply irregular as though bitten into. This characteristic of the cones distinguishes them from the cones of the Black Spruce—a tree much like its Red cousin. Red Spruces furnish the famous spruce-gum, much utilized in the country as chewing gum. The Red Spruce ranges from eastern Canada along the St. Lawrence River to New York, and southward along the higher mountains into Tennessee and North Carolina, although sparingly. In the cold northern regions, and in cold low swamps, its place is taken by the Black Spruce. The Cat, or White Spruce, is a similar tree, with a pungent odor of a catty, or skunky, nature. One of its less agreeable names is Skunk Spruce. It may be readily separated from the Red and Black Spruces by the whitish or silvery greenish characters of its needles, and by the above-mentioned distinctive odor, especially of the crushed or roughly handled needles. If branches are brought into a very warm room, this catty or skunky odor becomes very agreeable to some people and very disagreeable to others.

The very familiar Norway Spruce (the one called "pine tree" by so many people, and whose outline is so much used in art under this misnomer) is a common tree of dooryards, parks, cemeteries, and the like. It was introduced into this country from Scandinavia, and has become a very dignified and welcome feature of our domestic scenery. It is a very tall tree, with long, curved drooping branches. Its cones are cylindrical and elongated, and measure from four and a half to about seven inches in length.

Colorado Blue Spruce.   The western tree known best all over the United States is perhaps the Colorado Blue Spruce, or Silver Spruce, for the reason that it has become so widely used as an ornamental in parks and private grounds. It is a beautiful pale grayish-blue evergreen, and may be recognized wherever seen by the fact that it is the lightest colored of all our native spruces. For this reason it is often also called the Silver Spruce. It grows only about twenty-five to forty feet in height in the east, but in Colorado it sometimes attains a height of eighty-five to one hundred feet. The branches are horizontal, and the bluish leaves are layered in a definite horizontal plane. The bark is grayish-brown, rough and scaly when young, but on old trees it becomes deeply ridgy and furrowed. A peculiarity of this tree (and one which sometimes makes it not so desirable as a near neighbor to the house) is the fact that its needles emit a rather disagreeable, pungent odor—rather catty or skunky in character—especially when the foliage is stroked or bruised. This odor is similar to that emitted by our common White Spruce or Cat Spruce (a tree also called the Skunk Spruce in New England). The native haunts of the Blue Spruce are the Rocky Mountain region of Colorado and

eastern Utah, and northward to the region of the Wind
River Mountains of Wyoming.

Hemlock.   A very graceful, soft-appearing evergreen is
the Hemlock (Fig. 126), growing as a small shrubby tree,

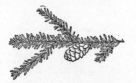

FIG. 126—Hemlock.

or to a forest giant of eighty feet or more, although such trees
are very rare in most parts of our country. It is usually seen
as a tree from twenty-five to forty feet. Its favorite haunts
are on the rocky ridges and slopes of mountains, as well as
on steep mountains and hillsides, and along the sides of cool
rocky ravines and deep valleys. Its trunk becomes cracked
into coarse, deep, grayish-brown ridges. Its branches are
long, slender, drooping, and graceful, and the tips are especially slender and pretty. The small needles are distinctive;
they are not cylindrical but are flattened and short, blunt,
and arranged on the twigs in one or two opposite rows.
They are a lovely clear, shining green above, but underneath are a softer green, and show a thin silvery median
line. They average a little less than half an inch in length.
The cones are ovoid, medium to light brown, with thin
rounded scales, and are from a half an inch to an inch long.
This lovely tree is found in eastern Canada, and in all the
provinces and states bordering the Great Lakes; also in New
England, and southward (becoming rarer as it goes) along
the Appalachians.

Balsam Fir.　A much-loved tree is the Balsam Fir (Fig. 127), one of the most commonly used for Christmas trees. It grows with a very graceful, erect, cone- or spire-like shape, often tapering out at its top into a long, slender, pointed steeple. It grows ordinarily to a height of about thirty-five feet, but may reach from forty to sixty feet in

FIG. 127—Balsam Fir.

the north. The branches are regular and spreading; the bark is grayish-brown and nearly smooth, and often is puffed out here and there with little brown blisters, filled with clear sticky resin, the "Canada Balsam" so much used in microscopical mounts. The bark of the older trees frequently is cracked up into scales. The leaves, or needles, commonly in two rows, are flat, usually blunt-pointed, a glistening dark green above and silvery green below. They range from one half to one inch in length. Since the needles possess no petioles (leaf-stems), their fall leaves the twigs smooth. The cones are borne erect and are sticky with exuded resin, which often collects in little glistening droplets, like jewels. When fresh, they are of a delicate pink-purplish color, and are from two to four inches in length. The cone scales are oblong and gradually fall off while the cones are still attached to the branches. The Balsam Fir (also called the Fir Balsam, or simply Balsam, or Fir) occurs throughout Canada, northern New England and New York, and along the higher reaches of the Appalachian Mountains as far south as Virginia, and westward through the Great Lakes region into northern Iowa.

Red Cedar.   Another attractive tree is the Red Cedar (Fig. 128). It occurs as a small tree, or sometimes as a shrub. Usually it develops a slender, pointed, spire-like top,

FIG. 128—Red Cedar.

and a rather fattish base, although sometimes, as when the trees grow in close ranks, it is tall, slender, and cylindrical with very little broadening at the base. On high elevated situations Red Cedars sometimes form mat-like growths. The wood is very fine-grained, reddish, or pinkish, or flesh-color, and very fragrant. For this reason it is often used to line closets, or trunks, or chests. It is also largely used in the manufacture of pencils. The bark is a grayish or light reddish-brown, and on old trunks cracks up into long narrow strips, which become soft and shreddy. The leaves, which are fragrant, are of two sorts: needle-like and spreading outward from the twigs, and scale-like and appressed closely against the twigs. They are dark green or a lighter green, but in winter may have a decided brownish tinge or even reddish. They measure something less than one-tenth of an inch in length. The very attractive little cones are berry-like in form, and about as large as a very small blueberry, light bluish in color. The Red Cedar (sometimes spelled Red-cedar) is a very common tree all along the wide coastal

zone of the eastern United States; it is not an inland tree to
any great extent. It grows on dry soils on low hills all along
our coast everywhere, and ranges from the south as far
north as southern Nova Scotia, Ontario, and North Dakota.

American Holly.   The Holly is a broad-leaved Evergreen, thus differing markedly from the Needle-bearing
Evergreens. Of the more than thirty species of holly growing wild or cultivated, the most familiar one is the American
Holly (Fig. 129), the scarlet "berried" evergreen of Christ-
mas-time. The holly is a shrub or tree with light gray or
brownish gray smooth trunk and widely spreading
branches. It may grow up to a height of fifty feet. The

FIG. 129—American Holly.

elliptical, leathery evergreen leaves are very spiny. In early
summer, small creamy white flowers appear in loose clusters
at the leaf-bases. Male and female flowers are borne on
separate trees, hence if one wishes to grow a holly tree for
its bright red fruit (which is a drupe not a berry), one must
plant male and female trees near one another, or else graft
a male branch on a female tree. The fruits are usually
scarlet, though some may be yellow. The close-grained
wood is used in cabinet work. The American Holly tree is
found in sheltered sandy and moist places from Massachusetts south to Florida and Texas.

LEAFY TREES OF THE EAST AND NORTH

Sugar Maple.   The maples are a large family of trees, highly valued as shade trees, as ornamentals, as sources of timber, and in one species, as a source of sugar. Their fruits are the well-known "maple-keys" or winged seeds. Their leaves are the commonest of all the leaves which fill our city streets in the fall with their dry, fragrant, rustling heaps. Maple trees are among the favorite trees as shade trees along our streets; in this respect they are rivals of the Elm. A common species and a much-loved one, is the Sugar Maple (Fig. 130). It is a desirable tree for its shade, its

FIG. 130—Sugar Maple.

lovely fall colors, and especially for its sweet sap which is boiled down into syrup and then sugar. It grows to a height of sixty to one hundred feet, with regularly-divided branches, which gives a perfect specimen a typical egg-shape. The twigs are green, smooth, and then become slightly rougher and a reddish-brown. The bark is light brown and smooth at first, but on older trees becomes broken up into coarse scales, or irregular long plates. In the fall the leaves become flesh-color, red, yellow, and purple. They are about three to six inches long. Sugar Maples, or Sap Maples, are cultivated in groves called "sugar bushes," and occur most commonly in hilly regions (especially in New England—Vermont in particular), and are said to be the most widely cultivated wild tree in eastern North America. They range from eastern Canada to Manitoba and southward.

Red Oak. In our area there are found about twenty-one different kinds of oaks. These are placed in two groups: the Red or Black Oaks, possessing leaves whose lobes are sharp and bristle-tipped, and the White Oaks, whose lobes are rounded, or which possess no bristles. The common Red Oak (Fig. 131) is one of our finest and stateliest of forest

FIG. 131—Red Oak.

trees. It reaches upward to a height of one hundred fifty feet. It has hard, smooth, grayish-brown bark, later cracking up into broad flat ridges. The branches are relatively few, high, stout, and spreading. The leaves are thin and hard, with five to eleven triangular lobes pointing toward the tip of the leaf. Each lobe has two or more bristle-tipped divisions. The leaves are a dull shining green above, rather paler and smoother below, and from four to nine inches in length. The fruit is an acorn, brownish-red, the cup covered with small, smooth, tightly-adherent scales. The Red Oak grows from eastern Canada to Kansas, Missouri, sparingly southward.

White Oak. The species of oak called the White Oak

(Fig. 132) may be recognized in the field by its leaves, which are obovate and deeply divided into three to nine coarse lobes, roundish at their tips and without the bristly

FIG. 132—White Oak.

points which the Red Oak has. The leaves may vary in form, but the character of bristleless lobes is constant. The White Oak is one of our most valuable trees. Its trunk is short and stocky and its branches large and stout, and often very wide-spreading. In the open country this tree assumes huge dimensions, very spready, and with a rounded or ovate form. The acorns are less than an inch long, and are seated firmly in a cup covered with firm, somewhat hairy little scales. White Oaks are found distributed widely from Maine and Ontario, westward through Minnesota, and thence southward. Where they grow in the open, they are such splendid trees that often they are spared by farmers or road-builders because of their great beauty.

Sweet Birch. Known also as the Cherry Birch, the Sweet Birch (Fig. 133) is a forest-dweller chiefly, reaching

FIG. 133—Sweet Birch.

a maximum height of seventy to eighty feet. It may be recognized by its bark, which is somewhat like that of the
cultivated cherry tree—dark brown with a decided reddish
tinge. On very old trunks the bark assumes a grayish or slaty
hue, with thick, rough, irregular plates. The twigs are covered with a smooth bright brown bark, which possesses a
very agreeable sweetish wintergreen flavor and is often
chewed by walkers in the woods. The leaf is somewhat
heart-shaped, but varies to ovate, and is toothed. It is from
two to six inches in length, green above, but below paler and
somewhat hairy in the angles of the veins. The Sweet Birch
ranges from Canada southward to Illinois and Tennessee.

Canoe Birch.   Also commonly called the Paper Birch
(and sometimes the White Birch), the Canoe Birch (Fig.
134) has a creamy-white bark of a papery nature. When

FIG. 134—Canoe Birch or Paper Birch.

this peels off (which it does readily) it exposes a thin bark
underneath which is tinged with brown, dull orange, and
sometimes fleshy-pink, or pinkish-yellow. There are several
varieties of this species. Our commonest form possesses
ovate, toothed leaves, smooth dull green above and slightly
hairy in the angles of the veins beneath. The Canoe or
Paper Birch ranges from Canada southward into New Eng-

land, northern New York, Pennsylvania, Indiana, Iowa, and Nebraska. In parts south of this region its place is taken by the Gray Birch—which, like the Canoe Birch, is also known as the White Birch (see below).

Gray Birch.   The Canoe Birch (which see above) may be distinguished from the Gray Birch (Fig. 135) by the fact that the latter bears, beneath the point where the branches

FIG. 135—Gray Birch.

emerge from the main stem, black triangular markings. The Gray Birch is also called the White Birch and the Poplar Birch. It is a small slender tree, sometimes reaching the height of thirty to thirty-five feet, but does not often attain its maximum height, since it is so frequently bent over and broken by heavy accumulations of ice. It grows on poor soils and in the edges of swampy lands. The bark is a dull chalky white, or dirty grayish-white, with the characteristic markings noted above. In young saplings the bark shows no trace of white, but it is a bright reddish-brown, changing to dull brown, then chalky brown, then gradually dull whitish, to white in the older trees. The leaf is triangular, with a flattish base and a rather elongated tip. It is smooth and shining, but a dull shade of green. This very common tree often grows in dense groves of small trees, and is found from eastern Canada southward through New York and

New England, becoming increasingly more common in the middle part of its range. It extends down into West Virginia and Delaware.

Beech.   A very distinctive tree, and one which the beginner can identify with ease from its very smooth, light bluish-gray (or almost silver or aluminum-gray) trunk and larger branches is the Beech (Fig. 136). The trunk is tall

FIG. 136—Beech.

and slender in the forest where the trees often grow together in a grove, but out in the open the tree has a short trunk and widely-spreading branches. The twigs are light green, smooth, and slender, and later turn to reddish-brown or brownish-gray. The leaves are borne in two rows on the long twigs, and the tips of the branchlets; later, on the older plants, they become clustered at the ends of the short twigs. They are ovate and elongated and narrowed at each end. In color they are bluish-green above, and shining yellowish-green below, softly hairy when new, and from one to four and a half inches in length. The fruit is a three-angled nut contained in a roundish, somewhat prickly bur. There are several cultivated forms of beech trees, well known. Some of these are the Copper Beech, with dark-colored coppery-green leaves; the European Beech, also with dark green leaves; and the familiar Weeping Beech, with slender drooping branches. Our native American Beech is found usually on rich uplands in the North, but also in the South in rather moist places everywhere. It ranges from Nova Scotia, Ontario, and Wisconsin southward.

American Elm.   The very familiar tree called the American Elm and also known as the White Elm (Fig. 137) is an embodiment of grace and beauty. Its trunk is tall,

Fig. 137—American Elm.

slender, and straight, and its branches are wide-spreading, often drooping at their tips. Trees in the open form a characteristic vase-shape, or wine-glass-shape, and may reach a height of 100 to 150 feet. The twigs are very slender and tough, smooth and green, sometimes hairy. The bark cracks up into broad, flat, scaly ridges, and is of a light grayish color, with no tinge of brown. The leaves are toothed, and either smooth or only lightly rough above; underneath they are slightly hairy, and a bit paler in color; their length is from two to six inches. The Elm is a tree of river valleys, and broad moist meadows and fields, particularly in New England, and ranges from Newfoundland westward to Manitoba and southward. The English Elm (also naturalized in this country) is similar to the American Elm, but is not typically vase-shaped. It has irregular rather rugged branches, stouter than those of our elm, which spread outward, rather crooked and not drooping. Altogether, while a more rugged muscular tree, it lacks the sweep and grace of the American Elm.

Chestnut.   This valuable, nut-bearing tree is one of our vanishing Americans! The rough-barked, massive trunks rise to a height of from sixty to over a hundred feet. The dull yellow-green leaves of the Chestnut (Fig. 138) are

FIG. 138—Chestnut.

toothed, and measure from five to ten inches in length. The showy yellow-green male flowers are clustered in long slender catkins; and the small inconspicuous female flowers occur in clusters at the base of the catkins. In autumn, round burs covered with long needle-like spines grow to a diameter of about two and a half inches. These split to release from one to three shiny, brown, sweet edible nuts. The wood is used for many purposes: for furniture, boxes, crates, poles, and fence-rails. These fine trees used to be very common from Maine south to Mississippi and west to Ontario and Michigan. They have now been almost eradicated by the Chestnut Blight. Much experimentation is now being carried on with marked success, in crossing the blight-resistant Asiatic chestnut with our native American species.

Tulip Tree.   Also called Whitewood or Yellow Poplar, the Tulip Tree (Fig. 139) is one of our tallest trees, frequently attaining a height of two hundred feet. Its trunk

FIG. 139—Tulip Tree.

is straight, and sometimes ascends upward for sixty to ninety feet without a branch. The bark is brownish-gray and smooth, but with age cracks up into a more or less regular network of thin ridges. On older trees these ridges are rough and deep. The leaves are very distinctive in shape, very smooth and shining, and measure from two to eight inches in length. The lovely showy flowers are very tulip-like, and are prettily marked with green and orange or deep yellow, and are from one and a half to three inches deep. The fruit, which is cone-like, remains attached to the twig for a year, and is from two to three inches in length. Tulip trees occur in rich woodlands from central New England westward to Ontario, and Wisconsin, and southward.

Sycamore.   Also known as the Plane Tree or Buttonball Tree, the Sycamore (Fig. 140) is one of our tallest trees, sometimes reaching the height of over 170 feet. The trees ordinarily seen, however, reach from about fifty to eighty feet. The branch system is massive and widely spreading, rising upward to form a rather broad, irregular top. The

FIG. 140—Sycamore or Plane Tree.

twigs are at first green, somewhat hairy, and then turn a
dark yellowish-brown; they are smooth, and in older
growths become dark gray. The bark is a reddish- or grayish-brown and cracks off in large and small irregular
patches, showing beneath the irregularly-shaped areas of
whitish, yellow, green, and gray which look like a map of
the shires of England in different colors. On very old large
trunks the bark breaks up into coarse, thin, scaly, dark
brown ridges. The leaves are peculiar and distinctive, somewhat maple-like in contour, and about four to nine inches
wide. Sometimes very large leaves may be found, exceeding
ten inches. They are tough and hard. The fruit is very distinctive, at first a round green ball, then turning a delicate
brown, and able to be shredded into a mass of fluff, bearing
the numerous seeds. They are about an inch in diameter,
or larger, when brown. These hang on the tree long after
the leaves have fallen, like a lot of little Christmas-tree balls.
This gives the tree one of its common names, Buttonball
Tree. Sycamores are found chiefly in low wet bottom lands,
along river courses, and occur from southern Maine (sparingly) and Ontario, to Nebraska and southwards.

White Ash.   A very large tree, very valuable for its timber, is the White Ash (Fig. 141). Its trunk is heavy,
straight, and looks like a huge column from a Greek temple,

FIG. 141—White Ash.

as it ascends upward. The branches are likewise large and ascending, not drooping at the tips. The twigs are greenish or yellowish-green, sometimes with an orange or flesh-colored tint; the older ones turn light brown, or brownish gray, and acquire a sort of polish. The bark is dark brown or dark brownish-gray, and cracks up later into a more or less regular network of firm, hard, deep ridges. The leaves, which are compound, measure about six to twelve inches or more in length. They are composed of five to nine ovate or elongate-ovate leaflets, light or dark green above, but a yellow-green or even silvery-green below, often slightly fuzzy on the veins. They are usually from two to six inches long. The winged fruit hangs in rather long branched clusters. This noble tree is very common on rich soils, in wet places, or low damp situations, from the Great Lakes region southward and eastward.

Black Willow.   The willows are a very large group of trees. The majority of them are more or less shrubby in nature; a few of them, however, becoming large trees. The tree forms occur usually with crooked, irregular branches, and their bark is broken into brown or dark grayish-brown irregular ridges. The most common of all our native willows is the Black Willow (Fig. 142). This is a shrub or small tree with clustered trunks (stems), and grows to a height of twenty to sixty feet. The top is very uneven and open (that is, not pointed or rounded or flat). The twigs are at first a reddish-brown, or sometimes grayish, but with age they turn much darker. The bark is a dark, almost blackish-brown,

FIG. 142—Black Willow.

and is broken up into flat broad ridges. On old trunks these become very rough and shaggy. The leaves are narrow and lanceolate in form, smooth above and somewhat hairy on the veins beneath. Their tips are long, curved, and graceful, and their color a cheerful bright green. This willow grows along low river and brook banks, and the low damp shores of lakes, and in low damp stream valleys. It likes to have its "feet in the water." Along lake shores it reaches out over the water as a sort of low fringe, in a very characteristic way. Often its long brown or yellowish-brown roots sweep into the water like masses of coarse hair. Its range is from southern Canada throughout the central and eastern states as far south as Colorado and across to Tennessee. In this same territory occur some thirteen different forms of tree-like willows. Some of these are: the Longleaf Willow, Weeping Willow, Pussy Willow, Balsam Willow, Peachleaf Willow, White Willow.

Sassafras.   There are only three species of these aro-

matic trees in the world; one of these is native to North
America, one to Asia, and one to the island of Formosa.
Sassafras (Fig. 143) attains a height of forty or fifty feet.

FIG. 143—Sassafras.

The aromatic bark is deeply furrowed and checkered. The
very variable leaves often mitten-shaped, are from three to
six inches in length. The loose drooping clusters of greenish
yellow male and female flowers are borne on separate trees.
The fleshy dark blue ovoid fruits about half an inch long
are borne on thick bright red stalks. Sassafras trees spread
by means of suckers, and often become a nuisance in fields
in our southern states. The wood is brittle and coarse-
grained. Sassafras tea, and oil of sassafras are made from
the thick juicy bark of the roots.

Black Locust, Yellow Locust, or Shipmast Locust.   Several species of locust trees and shrubs are native to America.
The common Black Locust (Fig. 144) is a tree growing
from forty to eighty feet high, with deeply furrowed, rough-
ridged bark. The twigs bear a pair of spines at the base of
each leaf. The compound leaves, eight to fourteen inches
long, are odd-pinnate, the seven to nineteen leaflets being

FIG. 144—Black Locust.

smooth and dark above but paler beneath. At the tip of each leaf is a notch and a whisker. Pendant showy clusters of fragrant creamy white flowers, four to eight inches long, are favorites of the honey bees. The flat brown pods, two to four inches in length, contain several kidney-shaped seeds. Black Locusts grow in woods and thickets from Nova Scotia and Ontario south to Georgia, Louisiana, and Oklahoma. Their very hard and durable wood is valuable for fence posts, railroad ties, and poles. This tree was introduced into Europe as early as 1600, where it is now naturalized.

Horse-Chestnut. These large, heavy spreading trees from forty to one hundred feet in height are planted for

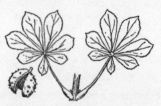

FIG. 145—Horse-Chestnut.

ornament and shade, and often escape from cultivation. The Horse-Chestnut (Fig. 145) was introduced into our country from Asia, and Europe, and is especially common in Greece. The dull brownish bark is thin and scaly, and the twigs are coarse and stout. In winter the large glistening sticky buds are very conspicuous. The leaves are compound and opposite, rough above, and lighter beneath; they are usually made up of seven leaflets, each from four to ten inches in length. Showy, erect flower clusters often a foot long appear in early summer. The individual flowers are white blotched with madder purple and yellow. The tree which bears the red flowers is a hybrid Horse-Chestnut. Similar to the Horse-Chestnut is the Ohio Buckeye, which is distinguished by its leaflets which are fewer and taper-pointed.

Butternut. The large stout tree called the Butternut (Fig. 146) reaches a height of thirty-five to eighty feet. Its trunk is rather short and stocky, and its branches heavy and spreading. Its top is broad and rather irregular. The

Fig. 146—Butternut.

branches are coarse and rough; when young they are rusty-hairy, and somewhat greenish, and sticky, but later they become reddish-brown or dull yellowish and smooth. On older trees the bark is cracked up into flattish, brownish-gray ridges. The leaf is compound, from one to two feet in length, and is made up of seven to fourteen oblong-lanceolate leaflets about one to two inches long. They are rough above but hairy beneath, and yellowish in color. The fruit is the delicious butternut with which all are familiar, of rich flavor and heavy with oil. The fruits grow in clusters of three to five cylindrical nuts, at first dull greenish and hairy, but later turning brown, the shell dryish but sticky and possessing sharply notched ridges. This very desirable tree is found from eastern Canada and Ontario southward through middle and eastern North America as far south as Colorado and Tennessee. It is similar to the Black Walnut which bears rounded instead of elongated nuts.

Shagbark Hickory. The familiar "Walnut" Tree of the North, well known for its delicious nuts, is also called the Shagbark Hickory (Fig. 147). It is a stately tree, with a firm straight column-like trunk and very strong muscular branches. The bark is at first smooth and brownish-gray or

FIG. 147—Shagbark Hickory.

even slate-gray, but later, in older trees it breaks up into large, thick, hard, curved plates which may be a foot long and four or five inches broad. These, adhering to the trunk

for a long time, give the tree its name of Shagbark. In the
more southern parts of its range the tree is better known
under the name of Scalybark. Hickory wood is exceptionally
hard, tough, and pliable, and is often used in the making
of bows for archery. The Indians used its wood for their
bows, and also for arrows. The leaves are compound, from
eight to fourteen inches long, and made up of five oblong-
lanceolate leaflets from four to seven inches in length. They
are dark yellowish-green, and finely toothed. The fruit is
a roundish nut, sometimes slightly flattened, white or
creamy in color, with a thin but very hard shell, sometimes
slightly ridged, and containing the delicious seed in two
halves. The nut is surrounded by a thick greenish (then
brown) husk, which easily separates completely into four
equal parts, like the slices of a melon. The Shagbark Hickory grows in river valleys and on low rolling hilly land, and
extends from southern Quebec and Ontario southward.

Linden.   Also called the Basswood, or Whitewood, and
in England the Lime Tree, the Linden (Fig. 148) is a large

FIG. 148—Linden.

forest tree with many slender branches which form a somewhat rounded or egg-shaped top. The bark is smooth, gray,
or brownish, and cracks up into deep ridges on the older

trunks. The leaves are very broad and thick, with coarse teeth, and are hairy in the angles of the veins beneath. They measure from three to six inches long, and even larger. In the spring the new tender leaves are very agreeable to the taste, and are often chewed by the walker in the woods for their mild, slimy consistency. When one is hungry a mouthful or two of leaves allays the hunger very well. The Basswood is found in rich soils in woodlands from eastern Canada and southern Quebec, to Ontario and Manitoba, and southwards.

Quaking Aspen. One of our common trees is the Quaking Aspen (Fig. 149), its leaves always aquiver. It grows to a height of about forty or fifty feet, although com-

Fig. 149—Quaking Aspen.

monly it is seen as a tree of only about twenty-five or thirty feet. It is a rather round-topped tree, and its branches are crooked and droop at their ends. The bark of young trees is smooth, thin, yellowish-brown or greenish, or sometimes greenish-gray, often showing longitudinal ridges which give it a rough appearance. Near the base of the trunks of old trees, the bark is distinctly ridgy and dark gray, or even blackish. The leaves are smooth and lustrous, but rather finely downy when new. They are about one and a half to four inches in length. A peculiarity of this tree is reflected in its name, for its leaves show a constant agitated quivering motion. This is because the stem or petiole of the leaf is flattened at right angles to the blade of the leaf itself. Watch the aspens carefully, and see if you ever notice one whose leaves are at rest! The Quaking Aspen is found in gravelly and sandy situations, and ranges all over Canada, and southward to Pennsylvania and Missouri. The Aspen belongs to the Poplar family, as does the Cottonwood of the Southwest.

Sweetgum. With spreading branches which form a rather symmetrical, narrow top, the Sweetgum (Fig. 150)

FIG. 150—Sweetgum.

reaches a height of thirty-five to seventy-five feet. The bark is recognizable from its deep narrow scaly ridges, and the twigs themselves develop one or more deep corky wings or thin ridges running along their length. These are unique. They are light yellowish-brown or light reddish-brown. The leaves also are distinctive, being beautifully star-shaped; they measure about two to six inches across. The fruit likewise is easily recognizable—a mildly prickly ball, brown in color, very decorative, clinging to the tree all winter. It measures about an inch in diameter. Sweetgums grow in damp or wet situations from central New England (rarely), westward to Illinois, and southward.

Hackberry, Sugarberry, or Nettle-Tree.   This is a medium-sized tree varying from twenty to one hundred and twenty feet in height. The trunks of the Hackberry (Fig. 151) range from light brown to gray, and are conspicuously

FIG. 151—Hackberry.

irregular with corky warts and ridges. The alternate leaves are bright green above, sometimes rough, paler beneath, and are from three to five inches long. They are sharply toothed, except the lower third, with three main veins from the base. With the expanding leaves, inconspicuous pale green flowers appear; the female ones being usually solitary in the axils of the upper leaves; and the male ones being in the leaf-axils near the bases of the branches. The fruit is about one-fourth of an inch long, orange-red to dark purple, one-seeded, sweet, and edible. Hackberry trees are grown for shade and for ornament. They grow wild from Quebec south to Florida and west to Idaho and New Mexico. They often bear abnormal bunches of branches called witch's brooms.

Black Cherry.   The largest of our native cherry trees, the Black Cherry (Fig. 152), grows to a height of eighty to one hundred feet, and sometimes even higher. The twigs have a green-yellow tinge, then become red, and finally reddish-brown. The bark is reddish-brown and smooth, and bears longitudinal streakings. On older trees it breaks up

FIG. 152—Black Cherry.

into irregular, rough, thick scales which are either reddish or dark grayish-brown. The leaves are somewhat thin-leathery and bear fine, incurved, blunt teeth. They are smooth and shining on their upper surface, and measure from two to six inches in length. The fruits hang in long clusters and are at first green, then bright red, then dark red —almost black—when ripe. To the taste they are usually agreeable, though tangy, but sweetish. They measure about half an inch or slightly less when ripe. The Black Cherry is also known as the Wild Cherry, but this is not a good name, for there are several species of wild cherries. It ranges from Nova Scotia and the Dakotas, southwards.

Shadbush, Serviceberry, or Juneberry.   There are many species of these showy shrubs and small trees, growing wild or cultivated from imports from Europe and Asia. The bark of the Shadbush (Fig. 153) is gray and smooth; the leaves, from two to four inches long, are woolly on the veins be-

FIG. 153—Shadbush.

neath. The conspicuous, pendant, white flowers are in clusters about two inches long, and appear before the leaves, making a pretty showing in early spring at just the time when the shad run up the streams to spawn. The small blue or purplish berry is very sweet and edible; but the birds usually find them first! The hard, heavy wood is used in fine cabinet work, for tool handles, and for canes. This tree is found wild from Maine and New Hampshire south to Georgia and Louisiana.

Flowering Dogwood.   A lovely tree, familiar to all who walk abroad in the spring woodlands, where its clusters of lovely white flowers (mostly a circle of modified leaves) attract every eye is the Flowering Dogwood (Fig. 154). The Dogwood is a small flat-topped tree, with the grayish branches bent upward in a characteristic way at their tips. The bark is at first smooth and light brownish in color, but on older trunks becomes broken up into black, irregular, squarish little blocks. The flowers of this tree are not well

understood. They are minute, greenish, and borne in small
clusters, the whole cluster being only about half an inch or

Fig. 154—Flowering Dogwood.

so across. These are the true flowers. Around this tight
cluster of small flowers there spread out a group of four
pink or white very showy leaflets with a notch in the outer
edges. These are what are commonly thought of as the white
petals of the "flower"—in reality they are modified leaves.
They spread out into a "flower" some three to four inches
across. The fruits are scarlet berries, in a tight cluster where
the minute flowers were. Sometimes these berries are an
orange, or even a yellowish, color. This lovely, striking tree
grows in loose open woodlands, or along the edges of
woods, commonly on hillsides, from southern Maine and
Ontario and increasingly numerous from Minnesota southwards.

Mountain Ash.   Also called Red-fruit, the Mountain
Ash (Fig. 155) is a rather small tree, famous for its heavy
clusters of brilliant, large coral-red berries—a striking sight
in the late summer and early fall. The bunches of berries are
numerous, and are the first thing one sees when coming
upon a tree. The tree is rather slender, with spreading
branches—a rather ragged-looking tree, often, with a narrow, loose, somewhat rounded top. The bark is grayish-
brown and smooth, and breaks up into plate-like scales on

FIG. 155—Mountain Ash.

older trunks. The inner bark is fragrant. The leaves, from six to ten inches in length, are compound, and made up of nine to seventeen leaflets, from one to three inches long and finely toothed. This beautiful tree is much prized as an ornamental, and may be found in gardens, parks, along roadways, and so on. In its wild state it occurs in moist rocky woodlands, often on mountainsides (whence its name) and also along the borders of swampy regions. It ranges from eastern Canada to Maine, Iowa, and in the higher mountains as far south as North Carolina. Despite its name it does not belong to the Ash Family.

Witch-Hazel.   There are two native species of Witch-Hazel (Fig. 156); one of them flowers in late autumn, and one flowers in winter or early spring. They are shrubs or small trees, growing from ten, fifteen, or twenty-five feet in height. The corrugated, dull olive-green leaves are about two to four inches long. The clusters of bright yellow flowers are borne in the leaf-axils; these are followed by brownish capsules which mature the following year, and forcibly eject the shiny hard seeds to a distance of from ten to forty-five feet. These hard seeds require about two years for their

FIG. 156—Witch-Hazel.

germination. A winter-flowering Chinese species of Witch-Hazel is often used for cultivation. The extract of the Witch-Hazel bark is widely used to soothe and refresh the skin.

Spicebush, Wild Allspice, Benjamin-Bush, or Benzoin. In the early spring, these shrubs, from seven to fifteen feet high, are among the very first shrubs to burst into flower. The bark of the Spicebush (Fig. 157) is a dull dark brown

FIG. 157—Spicebush.

and the leaves, deep green, are from two to five inches in length. The twigs, leaves, and berries are very aromatic. Small waxy greenish-yellow flowers cluster close to the twigs and are seen in very early spring before the leaves. The elliptical, berry-like fruits, about a quarter of an inch long, are bright scarlet, and very showy. These lovely shrubs grow in moist places from Maine and Ontario southwards into Florida and Texas. Cultivated species of Spicebush come from China, Japan, and Korea.

TREES OF THE WEST AND SOUTHWEST

Sequoias and Redwoods.   On the Pacific side of our country are also found those trees which are among the most remarkable plant growths of the world: the Big Trees, or Giant Sequoias (Fig. 158). These are said to be the oldest

Fig. 158—Big Tree or Giant Sequoia.

living things in existence. They are certainly among the bulkiest and weightiest of all living things.

One of these Giant Sequoia trees, of only average diameter and yet by no means the largest, when cut down, showed by the number of its annual rings that it had reached an age of about 2125 years! Many are much older. Some are said to be probably some seven thousand years old! Some of these Sequoias, of our Sequoia National Park, rise to a height of well over 300 feet, and show a circumference or girth of eighty-five to nearly one hundred feet. The trunks of Sequoias are very large and heavy at the base, and taper gradually upward. The great branches (many of them larger than the trunks of ordinary forest trees) begin to appear about one-half to two-thirds to the top of the tree. The bark is a deep cinnamon-red on the older trees, but a light purplish-red on the younger ones. These trees are members of the great Pine Family (Pinaceae), as their leaves and cones clearly show. The seeds are borne in very small oval cones. They are extremely small; it seems strange that from such tiny seeds can come so gigantic a vegetable growth! The Giant Sequoia, or Big Tree, or California Big Tree, as it is variously called, is scattered over somewhat restricted areas at elevations of 5,000 to 8,500 feet, on the western slopes of the Sierra Nevada Mountains. This region where the trees occur covers about fifty square miles and contains about twenty-six groves of trees. The largest of these groves, the Giant Forest, contains over 5,000 trees.

The California Redwood, another species of the Sequoia, is very similar, but grows only from about 185 to 285 feet high, or in rare cases perhaps nearly 300 feet. The bark of this tree, while a deep cinnamon-brown, shows a distinct grayish hue. The leaves are different from those of the Big Tree, being flat, sharply pointed, and stiff. It is not so long-lived as its larger cousin, reaching ages only from 1,000 to

1,400 years. It is of very great commercial importance; its
wood is extensively used in the manufacture of furniture,
doors, panellings, and general interior finishes. It ranges
from southwestern Oregon inland through the California
coastal region to Monterey County. It grows best in the region of the fog belts, climbing up on the western slopes of
the Coast Ranges to an elevation of about 2,500 feet.

Monterey Cypress.   A tree that is especially characteristic of the natural landscape along the coast of south-central
California is the Monterey Cypress (Fig. 159). This evergreen member of the great Pine Family grows to a height
of forty to seventy feet. It is attractively pyramidal in shape
when young, and in maturity it becomes flat-topped and

FIG. 159—Monterey Cypress.

even more picturesque, giving the impression of a tree
which is not very tall and which has the interesting contours
that we associate with dwarf, Japanese types of plant-
growth. The small, opposite, scale-like leaves are either
dark green or bright green. The cones may be oblong or
round. Like the larger trees of this region, the Monterey
Cypress lives to a great age.

Eucalyptus.   About orange and lemon groves, as well as
commonly along roadways and the streets of towns and

cities, one sees often the stately Eucalyptus trees (Fig. 160).
These arrest the attention at once by reason of their great
height and long straight trunks, their crowns of leaves tower-

FIG. 160—Leaves and blossom of Eucalyptus.

ing above all other trees in their vicinity. If one notices the
leaves one will see that they are unusual and very characteristic—long, narrow, leathery, somewhat one-sided, and so
held on the branches that their edges rather than their flat
surfaces are presented to the sun. The flowers are white, and
heavily filled with nectar. The Eucalyptus belongs to the
great Myrtle Family (Myrtaceae) of which there are some
300 or more species. Our Eucalyptus grows to 200 feet or
more; in rare cases the crown may reach an altitude of over
300 feet. The commonest of the Eucalyptuses of our country is the so-called Blue Gum, native to Tasmania and
Australia, although many other species are grown here.
They are, as you see, not American trees, but introduced
ones. Since they are trees which grow well in a warm moist
climate, they were early introduced into California and the
south. Another species, the Snow Gum, is able to withstand
temperatures considerably below freezing, and this grows
farther north and at much higher elevations.

Valley Oak. One of the most interesting trees of our Far West (on the Pacific Slope) is the Valley Oak. This is a tree which arrests the attention, not only because of the

FIG. 161—Leaf and acorn of Valley Oak.

beauty of its leaves and large acorns (Fig. 161), but also because it happens to be the largest of all our many western oaks. The trees grow in a curiously scattered fashion, unlike many woodland trees; the massive short-trunked individuals grow naturally rather far apart (as though thinned out), giving picturesque vistas through their open ranks. The Valley Oak may be recognized partly by this habit, and also by the grayish, very deeply furrowed bark. At the height of fifteen feet or a little more from the ground the trunk gives off large, heavy, rough-barked arching limbs, the drooping branchlets of which curve over and often sweep almost, if not quite, to the ground beneath. Altogether it is an unmistakable and striking tree. It is not noteworthy by reason of its height, since it seldom raises its crown more than ninety or a hundred feet from the ground—usually much less than this—nor is it remarkable for the diameter of its trunk, this seldom exceeding about four feet. Sometimes these trees show a tall, single, undivided trunk with the branches forming at the top a rather narrow, dome-like crown; but generally the trunk divides some fifteen feet or more from its base. The shape of the acorns is characteristic, usually a little asymmetrical, and of a pretty bright chestnut-brown color. Great quantities of these are produced and are matured in one season. The leaves are deeply lobate, prettily scalloped, and rather variable in form. They are a deep green and hairy on their upper surfaces, and lighter in color and a little less hairy on the under ones. The hairs are in the form of little bunches of stars. Not much is known about the age to which the Valley Oak may grow, but it is believed that they may attain between three hundred and four hundred years.

Cottonwood.   The familiar Cottonwood (Fig. 162) of the west and south is easily recognized as one of the numerous members of the Poplar Family. This is the common tree

FIG. 162—Cottonwood Tree.

on bottomlands and along stream courses everywhere. It is one of the largest of the poplars, and for this reason is sometimes referred to as the Giant Poplar, although Cottonwood and Carolina Poplar are its usual names. Sometimes the trees elevate their crowns to a height of over one hundred

fifty feet, although this is not usual, their normal height being from about sixty-five to ninety feet. The diameter of the
trunk ranges from three and a half to four feet, sometimes
six to seven feet. The bark is strongly seamed and ridged,
the ridges running together here and there. These are a
medium brown or light brown when the tree is young, and
a grayish-green when old, and smooth. The trunk of the tree
is straight and erect and stately, and the branches are not
drooping but ascend strongly upward. The twigs are a pretty
ochre yellow. The leaves are somewhat like other poplar
leaves, especially like those of the familiar imported Lom-
bardy Poplar, but not so broad and spreading at the base.
They are olive-green above, but paler and smooth beneath.
The flowers hang in long swinging loose catkins.

Joshua Tree.   Our southwest is the home of a great
many strange plant growths, but none is more strange than
the great, almost grotesque Joshua Trees (Fig. 163), which

FIG. 163—Joshua Tree.

one sees in Utah, and also in California. They are not
"trees," strictly speaking, for they are members of the Lily
Family. They are related to the Spanish Bayonets and
similar plants (Yuccas), and might be called gigantic tree-

like lilies. Their large woody trunks branch widely to form
a rather irregular head, and the end branches are twisted
and bent in various directions. They are densely covered
with compacted, stiff, pointed, narrow leaves. The name
was given to the trees (so it is said) by the early Mormons,
who when crossing the desert of Utah thought that the outstretched branches of the trees looked like the outstretched
arms of another Joshua, come to lead them out of the desert
to their promised homeland. The Joshua Trees often reach
the height of twenty-five to thirty feet, and the trunk may
ascend to fifteen feet before it branches. The leaves may
reach the length of about nine or ten inches.

Giant Tree Cactus.   On the mesas and on the rocky
slopes of the mountains of Arizona (and very sparingly in
Mexico and in the Colorado River valley country of California) one sees the tall, very striking, much-ribbed Saguaro
Cactus—also often called Suwarro, or Giant Tree Cactus
(Fig. 164). The species is practically confined to Arizona,
and many of the individuals are now preserved in the Sa-

FIG. 164—Giant Tree Cactus or Saguaro Cactus.

guaro National Forest, near Tucson, the rocky slopes being covered with a splendid forest of their huge candelabra. This is the largest and most spectacular of all our western cacti, its tall fluted columns often rising to a height of twenty to forty feet from the ground. The flutings on the trunks alternate with lengthwise grooves between. As the storage tissues of the plant fill up with water, after the very infrequent rains of the desert, the trunk increases in diameter and becomes taut and plump, the ridges or flutings flattening out and the hollows disappearing. It is said that these plants can live for a period of three years without a single drop of extraneous water. As the water in the storage tissues is used up, the plant shrinks, the ridges reappear, move closer together, and the Saguaro reassumes its characteristic fluted appearance. The Saguaro grows very slowly; at the age of fifty years it is only about fifteen feet in height; even a ten-year-old plant may be less than a foot high. Some plants, therefore, between the heights of thirty and forty feet, must be at least two hundred years old. The flowers are remarkable, not only because they are borne high in the air at the summits of the stems, but also because they blossom for one night only, closing during the morning of the following day. They are large and waxy white in color, and contain thousands of stamens surrounding the central pistil. This flower, most appropriately, is the official State Flower of Arizona.

PALMS AND OTHER TREES OF THE SOUTH

Live Oaks. From Virginia, all along the coast and coastal states as far as Texas, and increasing in numbers southward, one sees large spreading evergreen trees (with broad leaves, however) which, one notes with surprise, bear acorns. As you look up into the tops of some of these trees you remark that they must be at least fifty or sixty feet high. These are the famous so-called Live Oaks (Fig. 165)—

FIG. 165—Leaves and acorns of Live Oak.

called live because they are evergreen, or always "alive". The trunk diameter of some of these trees attains a size of six or seven feet. In the open lands you will notice that the trees form a symmetrical broad-topped figure with very widely-spreading limbs, and drooping, silvery gray branchlets. The small evergreen leaf is entirely without lobes (such as most of our oaks show), and without teeth. Sometimes the edge of the leaf is perceptibly undulating. The leaf is from two to four inches long, and is a dark olive green color above, and pale and somewhat hoary below, and finely hairy. The tree bears its flowers in March and April, and the acorns which follow are small and a dark chocolate-brown. The nuts are not edible. The Live Oak is found mostly in dry soils, and is often associated with the Palmettos. Its wood is extremely hard, heavy, and close-grained; it is difficult to work and often turns the edges of tools. But it is a lovely light brown wood, and takes a high polish. For this reason it is used as interior finishing for fine ships. This remarkable wood weighs sixty pounds to the cubic foot and is therefore the heaviest wood of all our native oaks. The Live Oak reaches its greatest development in our south Atlantic states, and in the interior of Texas is sometimes reduced to the proportions of a mere shrub. In North Carolina it is found commonly near the coast, on sandy soils, associated with two other species of oak, the Water Oak and the Willow Oak. From these it may be distinguished by its bark and limbs. The bark of the trunk is a very dark brown, rough, deeply furrowed with ridges, and the branches of the tree are a much grayer brown.

Mistletoe.   One often sees in our southern and southwestern states, high up among the branches of trees, large roundish green clumps of twigs and foliage, looking like great nests of some large bird. These are not nests, but are clumps of Mistletoe (Phoradendron) (Fig. 166). There is another Mistletoe, called the Dwarf Mistletoe (Arceuthobium), which grows similarly in spruce trees in the woods

FIG. 166—Mistletoe growing on branch of its host tree.

and swamps of our northernmost states and Canada. This also produces large bunches of twigs and leaves, but not of itself, for it is a tiny plant; the twigs and leaves are those of the spruce itself. But the common Mistletoe, the one which is familiar to people at least in the stores and in homes during the Christmas Season, is a parasitic plant; that is, it grows in the wood of its host tree and absorbs its nourishment therefrom. Usually many of these plants grow together, and are much branched. This little woody shrub (for such it is) builds up its rather fleshy stems on a tough solid woody axis, and bears thick, fleshy, or softly-leathery light green leaves. These come off the stem in opposite pairs, and in their axils, or angles, of the stem are borne the clusters of small, delicate, yellowish flowers. If you look at one of these flowers you will see something unusual about it—that is, that the flower is composed entirely of sepals; it has no petals. After the flowers are fertilized they produce the little berries, waxy-white and thickly clustered. These make the plant pretty for Christmas decorations. The Mistletoe is distributed all over the southeastern and central part of our country, from southern New Jersey to Indiana, and southward to Florida, Texas, New Mexico.

Pecan. These large, slender trees sometimes rise to a height of seventy to one hundred seventy feet; and in our country bear a crop of nuts estimated to be about twenty million pounds annually. The thick, brownish or grayish bark is deeply furrowed, ridged and cracked. The compound leaves of the Pecan (Fig. 167) are deep yellow-green, from twelve to twenty inches long, and bear from nine to nineteen sickle-shaped smooth leaves. In the spring the flowers appear in the axils of the leaves; clusters of small female flowers and pendulous male catkins about five or six

FIG. 167—Pecan.

inches long. The elongate, paper-shelled nuts are enclosed in a thin husk. Some pecan trees bear sweet, some bitter nuts. They both grow wild in the Mississippi Valley and in Mexico, but are now widely cultivated all over the South as well as in California. The wood is used for boxes, crates, and furniture. They are favored in the smoking of meats, to which the term "hickory-smoked" is correctly applied, as the Pecan is a member of the Hickory family.

Bald Cypress. Common in our southern swamps are the Cypresses (Fig. 168), particularly notable for the peculiar "knees," often a foot in diameter, which rise up conspicuously from the roots to a height of several feet above the swampy ground or the water. These are developed

FIG. 168—Cypress Twig.

from the large roots of the tree. From these roots also strong
hold-fasts are sent down, penetrating the earth deeply,
anchoring the trees and their "knees" firmly in their soggy,
muddy beds. This tree is a member of the Pine Family
(Pinaceae), as a glance at its leaves shows. The leaves are
somewhat like those of our common hemlock in form and
arrangement. They are light yellow-green on both their
upper and under sides. Those on the flowering twigs are
awl-shaped and overlapping. The little cones are rather unusual in shape, being almost spherical. They are a pretty
tannish-brown and about an inch in diameter—quite small
for so large a tree, for the cypress grows to a height of fifty
to eighty-five feet, with trees of one hundred fifty feet often
seen in favorable locations. The trees are often completely
surrounded with water, from which the trunks rise perfectly
straight and perpendicular up to a height of forty feet or so
without a single branch, this giving the tree a stately and
majestic appearance.

The species found commonly in the swamps from the
southern portion of Delaware south all along the coastal
zone and around the Gulf of Mexico, is known as the Bald
Cypress. The wood of this tree is very valuable. It is straight-
grained and easily worked, and lighter than White Pine. It
is a pretty brown color, varied near the roots with areas of
rich blackish-brown. It is very commonly used in exterior
and interior finishings of buildings, doors, sashes, and the
like. For the panelling of walls it is quite the equal in beauty
of some of the much more expensive imported hardwoods.
The Bald Cypress grows only very slowly. The oldest trees
in our southern swamps—those with trunks of a diameter
of only about two feet or so—are said to be about two hundred years old. In these old patriarchs, the upper branches

are horizontal, but the lower ones are drooping, the lowest ones very much so.

Palmetto.   A common palm along our southern coast is the Palmetto (Fig. 169) which is well known since it is the emblem of the State of South Carolina. The palms may be recognized among all other trees by the tall unbranched trunks with great crowns or fans of leaves falling gracefully

Fig. 169—Palmetto.

from a central point. The Palmetto of our south is also known as the Cabbage Palm, Sabal, or American Palmetto Palm. You will see it growing some twenty to forty or fifty feet high, and attaining a diameter of trunk, near the base, of two feet or so. The leaves are sometimes nearly five feet long. The wood of the Palmetto is very valuable in the building of ships, for it is not attacked by the so-called Ship-worm (which bores into old, soaked wood). The basal part of the broad leaves is used for fans. The fruit is not edible. The flowers are often noticed with surprise and pleasure. They occur in enormous clusters—of thousands—and hang down from among the crown of leaves. The name palmetto is applied also to other kinds of palms in our country. Some of these are the Blue, Dwarf, and Saw or Scrub Palmettos

—the low-growing species so commonly found along the low coastal regions of our southern states, as well as further inland, and in the West Indies. The Dwarf Palmetto is peculiar in that it has no stem.

Royal Palm. Among the large palms found in our South are the tall and stately Royal Palms (Fig. 170), whose

Fig. 170—Royal Palm.

leaves are different from those of the Palmetto in that they have no central broad palm-of-the-hand form, but are more like long stout feathers or plumes. Palms are especially graceful when the wind is blowing their long plume-like leaves in one direction.

Date Palm. Another palm, seen in California, Arizona, and Texas as well as in Florida, is the Date Palm (Fig. 171), an erect species which attains about one hundred feet and bears the edible fruits for which it is named. It is crowned with a feathery cluster of large leaves and bears, besides the fruits, small yellow flowers of a leathery texture.

Coconut Palm. A great many more palms than one

FIG. 171—Date Palm.

might at first suppose are grown in the United States. There are, in fact, more than two hundred species now growing in our country. One of the common Florida species is the Coconut Palm (Fig. 172), which bears the coconuts that

FIG. 172—Coconut Palm.

we eat. It grows to a height of fifty to one hundred feet, with graceful leaves that are twelve to eighteen feet long, composed of leaflets, which are two to three feet long.

Guide to Minerals, Rocks, and Soils

This book deals with the flowers and trees and plants which we find when we walk about in the country. The wild flowers and trees and other plants which we have discussed all derive their nourishment from the soil in which they grow. In looking for and observing plant life, we are certain to notice the soil and the rocks which we pass along the way. We therefore conclude our book with a section on the minerals and rocks and soils which we are most likely to see and to want to identify.

COMMON MINERALS

Quartz. One of the commonest minerals of the earth's crust is Quartz (Fig. 173). It is the "glassy mineral." It is

FIG. 173—Quartz crystals.

not hard to identify in any form. The crystals are found in crevices in rock, usually, or inside of hollow cavities. They are six-sided (hexagonal) little columns, with six-sided pyramids at each end, or more usually at one end only, often much crowded together, which crowding more or less distorts their form. The crystals are clear, glassy, and colorless when pure. If there are other mineral impurities present, then they may be of various colors and lustres. Quartz is a very hard mineral, no matter what its color or texture; it is seventh in the "scale of hardness" for minerals. There are ten grades of hardness. Talc is No. 1 and the diamond is No. 10. Some appreciation of what this hardness scale means may be gained by remembering that the fingernail is about No. 2, and the blade of a good pocket knife is about No. 6.

The different forms of quartz that one sees commonly are the following: (1) Rock Crystal, described above—the pure clear colorless variety, often used when cut to imitate diamonds; (2) Milky Quartz, which as its name implies is opaque, white, or light cream color, and milky in appearance; (3) Smoky Quartz, which is clouded, "smoky," and usually light brown to gray in color; (4) Citrine, a lovely clear yellow quartz, used often as cut stones, in which form it is known as False Topaz; (5) Amethyst, the well-known purple or lavender species of quartz, a valuable gem-stone when clear, pure, and of good color, and in nature often found lining crevices of rocks; (6) Rose Quartz, a clear or a milky variety of quartz, tinted with light pink, flesh-color, or with shades of rosy red; (7) Aventurine, a quartz which encloses tiny scales of mica (which see on page 164), or minute flecks of an iron mineral called hematite, which gives the mass a scintillating or sparkling or spangly appearance; (8) Prase, a lovely green variety of quartz, its color being due to the inclusion of thin, minute, fiber-like crystals of a green mineral called actinolite; (9) Cat's Eye, another variety in which there are enclosed silky fibres of the mineral, Asbestos, and which, when cut parallel to these fibers, produces an opalescent effect, like the shining of a cat's eye —brown, yellowish, yellowish-gray, or various hues of green (and not to be confused with the famous Oriental Cat's Eye, which is not quartz, but a much harder mineral known as Chrysoberyl); (10) Chalcedony, a quartz which may be partly clear, or very opaque, and sometimes banded, but chiefly characterized by its waxy appearance (Flint, a kind of chalcedony with impurities which gives it a brownish color, is found as nodules of various sizes usually imbedded in limestone); (11) Agate, a banded variety of quartz with pretty bands of various colors, and a glassy lustre, not waxy (Onyx is one kind of agate in which the bands are alternately black and white); and (12) Bloodstone, which, as its name indicates, is a quartz of the deep red color of blood and which is a stone that is often used in gentlemen's rings.

Feldspar.   Like quartz, the Feldspars (Fig. 174) are one of the commonest, in fact, the commonest, of the earth's minerals, and enter into the composition of many of the

FIG. 174—Feldspar.

rocks. Feldspars make up about sixty per cent of the crust of the earth. There are some five different kinds of feldspars, but they agree in being white, creamy, pink, light brown, or gray. They are not as hard a mineral as quartz, being about

No. 6 in the scale of hardness. The best places to see feldspars are in the very common rocks called Granite (which
see on page 166), where they form whitish or creamy
patches in the rock, with a shining, sometimes a silky or
satiny luster. In the commonest, or gray granites, the feldspars are of the colors just mentioned, but in pink granite
(or the deeper so-called red granites) it is the colors of the
feldspar which give the colors to the rocks. Feldspars are
never clear like quartz, but are opaque, milky, satiny in
appearance, and split along flat planes.

Mica. Nearly everyone is familiar with Mica (Fig.
175). The commonest kind is the White Mica, or Muscovite. This occurs in the rocks as crystals which are flat,

FIG. 175—White Mica.

shining, and easily split up into very thin, tough leaves,
often almost clear and transparent. Good White Mica is
often used as "glass" in the doors of stoves, where it is called
Isinglass. Its mineral name is Muscovite. Black Mica, known
as Biotite, is similar in form, but is a very dark gray, or
grayish-brown. In thin leaves it is of these colors, but in
thick crystals is black. Both kinds are often seen as little
shining flecks and larger flakes in granite. White Mica is
about No. 2 in the hardness scale; Black Mica is a little
harder, about 2½ or 3. Amber Mica, also called Coffee, or
Yellow Mica, is a mineral called Phlogopite. Its names sug-
gest its colors. It sometimes occurs as a dull reddish min-

eral. This is the kind of mica most largely used in electrical work.

Calcite. Another common mineral is Calcite (Fig. 176). This is somewhat like quartz in its general appear-

FIG. 176—Calcite.

ance, but since it is not as hard as quartz, it does not have the sparkling, glassy, almost diamond-like appearance. Its hardness in the scale is only No. 3, and hence it is easily scratched with the point of a knife. This is an excellent way of distinguishing it from quartz. Since its crystal form varies greatly, this mode of determination is very helpful. Often the crystals will not be perfectly clear, but have a dull look. This is the mineral which is largely responsible for limestone, this rock being made up of a mass of shell material, derived from Calcite. When limestone is pressed and heated in the earth's layers it becomes Marble. Natural chalk is a mass of soft white limestone. This is not the "chalk" of the classroom, which is a commercial product made from another mineral called Gypsum.

COMMON ROCKS

Rocks are made up of minerals. Some rocks are solidified and cooled liquid (just as some candy is solidified and cooled liquid). Other rocks are simply pressed, heated, and cemented particles of previously ground-up rocks. The first kind of rock is known as igneous (that is, fire-formed) rock; the second kind, as sedimentary (or laid-down) rock. Igneous rocks are made in the so-called "bowels" of the earth, that is, far below the crust where all is very hot. Then they have been thrust up by various forces. Sedimentary rocks were originally deposited in layers at the bottom of seas, ponds, lakes, and so on, by streams which brought down worn rocks from the land, in the form of sands, muds, and the like. Wind sometimes is the carrying agent.

Granite.   The commonest form of igneous rock, and one which may be seen over wide areas of country, is Granite (Fig. 177). It is a combination of quartz, feldspar, and

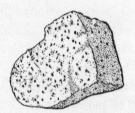

Fig. 177—Granite.

mica, sometimes with the admixture of other minerals. The size of the different minerals composing granite varies greatly. Very coarse granite is called Pegmatite. A granite-like rock lacking the quartz mineral is known as Syenite. It closely resembles granite. Gneiss is a banded granite. Pink granite, gray granite, yellow granite, red granite, and so forth, owe their colors to the colors of the included feldspars. When a great deal of feldspar is seen in granite—when the crystals are very large and numerous—one may be sure that this is a very weak, easily broken kind of granite.

This is often called "rotten granite." As one can see, it is not a good sort of granite to use as tombstones, or in buildings.

Sandstone. Nearly everyone is familiar with Sandstone (Fig. 178). It is an extremely common rock. It is found in layers, often seen projecting from railroad cuts, or in cuts

FIG. 178—Sandstone.

made through hillsides along big highways. The layers may be very thin or very thick. Sandstones may be very fine grained or very coarse. If one looks closely at a piece of sandstone, one can see (often with a naked eye, but very well with a simple hand-lens) the little individual grains of sand of which it is composed. Sandstones are simply deposits of sand, laid down in layers by water or wind, and then pressed and heated and fused together. Sandstones are much prized for building materials when they are fine-grained and well cemented. They split easily along their parallel planes, called bedding planes.

Conglomerate. Along cuts in railroads and other roads, one often sees what appear to be banks of gravel, with sand, little pebbles, and bigger stones, sometimes more or less

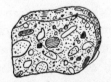

FIG. 179—Conglomerate.

rounded, all mixed together. On striking this bank with a hammer, or throwing a stone against it, one is surprised to find it a very solid rock indeed. This is called Conglomerate (Fig. 179). Another very descriptive name for it is Pudding Stone. It was made in a similar way to sandstone.

Shale and Slate.   Quite alike in general form are Shale and Slate. Both are rather fine-grained (slate very much so), and both split easily along horizontal planes. Shales (Fig. 180) are only solidified muds. They are not very hard

FIG. 180—Shale.

rocks, as a rule, and are usually quite friable (splittable, fragile, breakable). They are sedimentary rocks. Slates, somewhat like them, are much harder, finer grained, and split much more evenly and flatly. Slate results from the heating and pressing, deep in the earth's crust, of masses of shale. As a building stone, shale is of very little use; but slate is widely used, principally in the form of shingles. Very thick slabs of slate are used as door-stones, or in sidewalks.

COMMON SOILS

Rocks and minerals are not very much exposed on the surface of the earth; usually they are covered with a layer of soil. Soil is merely rock, broken up in large pieces, or pulverized into small ones. Often these soils are mixed with decaying vegetable material, as for example in a forest, where the dark soil is made up of pulverized rock material plus rotting leaves, twigs, ferns, mosses, liverworts, fungi, and the like. Soil is moved about over the surface of the earth, being carried by running water, or by wind, or sliding down steep slopes, urged by gravity, frost action and so forth.

It is not difficult to recognize the common kinds of soils. The kind we have been speaking of, mixed with decaying plant materials, is known as loam. In swamps, where the plant material forms a large proportion of the soil, so that it is a dark brown (sometimes black) it is known as peat. Peat is often so largely composed of pressed vegetable material, accumulated through long ages, that it can be cut into blocks and burned. In this form it is often called "turf." When peat is pressed down far into the earth and heated, it forms coal. Other kinds of soils, such as clay, loess, sand, and gravel, are formed from rocks and minerals alone.

Clay.   Everyone is familiar with Clay. It is firm, heavy, fine-grained, and when wet is tenacious and able to be moulded. In this respect is differs from all other soils. Its particles are very minute indeed, the finest to be found in any soil, and measure on the average about one 25-millionth of an inch in diameter. Clay may be found often in the bottoms, and on the sides of brooks and rivers, where these have cut channels through it. Clays are of various colors, the commonest color being gray. Clay is often found in large extensive layers, where it is mined. According to its commercial uses, the different kinds of clays are known as Fire Clay, Stoneware Clay, Sewer-pipe Clay, Brick Clay (the familiar reddish variety), Paving-brick Clay, and so on. Very fine lovely clays of different colors are used in making pottery and chinaware. Adobe is a kind of clay, of an impure, muddy sort, much used in the western parts of the United States, especially by the Indians, in making building bricks. These are not baked, but dried hard in the sun. Loess is a rather fine-grained clay-like material, with angular bits of sand, flakes of mica, and more or less limy materials. It is thought to be transported and deposited by wind. It sometimes forms great cliffs along wide river-valleys.

Sand. The kind of soil we call sand is a mass of loose fine particles of rock or of some mineral, the particles being from the size of a small garden pea down to fine bits about $\frac{1}{500}$ of an inch in diameter. Sand may be composed of various sizes of particles, but usually the particles are roughly about the same size. Oftentimes the sand consists of but one kind of rock or mineral, and oftentimes of two or more kinds. Sands made up of limy particles are called calcareous sands. They are whitish or cream color, usually, and are found abundantly along the seashore. Along the shore, also, are found bands, or larger deposits of greenish sand. If one looks at this through a lens one sees that it is made up of minute fragments of ordinary quartz, mixed with a dark green mineral known as glauconite. Some other very light green sands are mixed with a light clear apple-green mineral called olivine. Take a little hand lens with you the next time you visit the seashore. Put a few grains of sand in the palm of your hand, and examine them with the lens. Pure white sands, so commonly seen along the shore, are made up largely, if not almost wholly of quartz. The so-called "glass sand" is made up of pure quartz, and is used as one of the chief components in the making of glass. Very dark sand called "black sand," often found in narrow ridges and bands along the seashore, is made up largely of the black mineral magnetite. Red sand is white quartz sand with a large admixture of ground-up garnets. The so-called quicksands are deposits of extremely fine sand mixed with a good deal of clay. The clay enables this type of sand to hold a great deal of water, so that the whole mass is unstable and "mushy," and will not support the weight of a man, or sometimes even a dog. If the bed of quicksand is deep enough, it allows the man or other animal to sink into it gradually until suffocation and death result. The more the unfortunate creature struggles, the sooner he sinks below the surface. This is the reason for the name quicksand. Quicksands are often found at one end of small lakes. They are usually labelled, as a warning to picnickers or bathers.

Gravel. The name Gravel refers to a mass of loose material composed of sand and rock fragments, the pieces usually more or less rounded by water action, and all dumped down together without any sorting. The size of the pieces in gravel vary from very large boulders to very small pebbles and sand grains. All sorts of rock and mineral fragments are found in gravel: quartz, granite, sandstone, shale, and so forth. Gravels are common all along the northern borders of the United States where the glaciers have been. They are deposited in old deltas, outwash plains, and the like, and are exposed to view when railroads or highways make cuts through them. Gravels are valuable in the mixing of concrete, for road-ballast, drainage projects, and the like.

Wood-soils. Soils of various kinds, known as Wood-soils, are overlain with deposits of decaying leaves, ferns, twigs, mosses and liverworts, lycopodiums. This gives them a rick dark color—deep brown to black often. These soils support a very rich growth of plant life.

Peats and Mucks. In swampy regions one finds Peats and Mucks. They are like wood-soil, but are much blacker, heavier, and hold a large amount of water. They are the result of the growth and decay of marsh plants over a period of many thousands of years. When very black and solid they are cut into blocks, and burned as peat, or "turf."

———

Index

Quaking aspen, 136
Quartz, 161–163
    agate, 163
    amethyst, 162
    aventurine, 162
    bloodstone, 163
    cat's eye, 163
    chalcedony, 163
    citrine, 162
    milky quartz, 162
    prase, 162
    rock crystal, 162
    rose quartz, 162
    smoky quartz, 162
Queen Anne's lace, 49

Rattlesnake plantain, 93
Red-capped lichen, 15
Red-fruit, 141
Redwood, 144
Reed-mace, 36
Roadsides, wild flowers of, 46–77
Rockcap fern, 21
Rock crystal, 162
Rockfern, 21
Rock polypody, 21
Rock rose, 100
Rock tripe lichen, 14
Rocks, 165–168
Rose-mallow, swamp, 37
Rose quartz, 162
Rose, rock, 100
Rose, wild, 55
Rosette lichen, 13
Round-leaved sundew, 41
Royal palm, 159
Rue anemone, 84
Running pine, 16

Sabal, 158
Saguaro cactus, 151
St. James's weed, 67
St. John's-wort, 75
Sand, 170
Sandstone, 167
Sassafras, 130
Saw palmetto, 158
Saxifrage, early, 90
Scouring rush, 18
Selfheal, 64

Senecio, 104
Sequoia, 144
Serviceberry, 139
Shadbush, 139
Shagbark hickory, 134
Shale, 168
Shepherd's purse, 66
Shipmast locust, 131
Silkweed, 74
Silver leaf, 39
Silverrod, 71–72
Skunk cabbage, 34
Slate, 168
Smartweeds, 61
Smoky quartz, 162
Snow gum, 147
Soapwort, 76
Soils, 168–172
Solomon's seal, 87
    false, 88
Sorrel, wood, 89
Spanish bayonet, 150
Spanish moss, 106
Spicebush, 143
Spiderwort, 40
Spikenard, false, 91
Spirogyra, 27
Spotted cranesbill, 86
Spotted wintergreen, 95
Spring beauty, 81
Spring cress, 91
Spring welcome, 35
Spruce, 112–115
    black, 113
    Colorado blue, 114
    Norway, 114
    red, 113
    skunk, 113
Star of Bethlehem, 44
Starry campion, 58
Steeple bush, 54
Stink horn, 10
Stinking Benjamin, 83
Stonewort, 28
Strawberry, wild, 54
    wood, 54
Streams, lowly plant life of, 27–29
Succory, 51
Sugarberry, 138
Sugar maple, 119